# THE POETRY OF JAYANTA MAHAPATRA

Fourth Revised and Enlarged Edition

# THE POETRY OF JAYANTA MAHAPATRA

Fourth Revised and Enlarged Edition

Bijay Kumar Das

Published by

**ATLANTIC**

**PUBLISHERS & DISTRIBUTORS (P) LTD**

7/22, Ansari Road, Darya Ganj, New Delhi-110002
Phones : +91-11-40775252, 40775214, 23273880, 23275880
Fax: +91-11-23285873
Web: www.atlanticbooks.com
E-mail: orders@atlanticbooks.com



Printed & bound in India by Atlantic Print Services

*For My Parents*

*Whose Love*

*I Can't fathom*

# Preface to the Fourth Edition

Jayanta Mahapatra, the best known Indian English poet, both at home and abroad, happens to be the most prolific poet as well, with seventeen volumes of poems to his credit. Two of his latest volumes of poems, *Bare Face* (2000) and *Random Descent* (2005) appeared in the twenty-first century. Added to these two books of verse, his prose collection, *Door of Paper* appeared in 2007. In the fourth edition of my book, I have added a new chapter on his latest poetry and included his interview to me.

I have enjoyed reading his poetry and given my own interpretations of his poetry in the light of recent theories of criticism. I would be glad if this book helps the readers, researchers and teachers of our country to understand Mahapatra's poetry and appreciate it. The bibliography, as usual, is updated.

Last but not least, I am thankful to M/s Atlantic Publishers and Distributors (P) Ltd., New Delhi, particularly to its Chairman, Dr. K.R. Gupta for bringing out the fourth edition of the book in record time.

**Bijay Kumar Das**

# Preface to the First Edition

Jayanta Mahapatra has emerged as one of India's leading Indian English poets in recent years. He has won recognition both at home and abroad. He is now read all over the English speaking world. I have greatly enjoyed his poetry. Here, I make a humble attempt to interpret his poetry for those who seek an introduction to it. I hope this book will be useful to scholars and teachers who do research on Jayanta Mahapatra.

I would like to thank Professor P. Lal, a distinguished critic and pioneering Indian English poet, for undertaking the publication of this book.

**Bijay Kumar Das**

# Contents

# Introduction

# 1

ONE of the most widely known and published Indian English poets of our time is Jayanta Mahapatra. Like Nissim Ezekiel and A.K. Ramanujan, he is widely read and discussed both at home and abroad. But unlike Ezekiel and Ramanujan, Mahapatra is difficult to read for obscurity, complexity and allusiveness in his poetry. He is rather in the company of Shiv K. Kumar and Keki N. Daruwalla, in creating contrive images and learned vocabulary that immediately set him a class apart from most of his contemporaries. At the same time, in his desire to acclimatize an indigenous tradition to English language, and create a new Indian English idiom, he shares some of the concerns of the well-known Indian English poets of our time. Therefore, to study Jayanta Mahapatra in isolation seems to be a difficult task, especially when he has influenced a number of contemporary Indian English poets and brought recognition to this new poetry by winning the firstever award by the National Akademi of Letters for his book of verse, *Relationship* in 1981. In order to study his poetry in its proper perspective, one should take the background and development of Indian English poetry into consideration to arrive at a balanced judgment. That is why, I take the background of Indian English poetry into consideration to facilitate my evaluation of Jayanta Mahapatra as a contemporary Indian English poet.

The place and status of Indian English poetry before and after Independence are open to debate. There are people representing diametrically opposite views on the achievement of this poetry in general. One group outrightly condemns the poetry written before 1947 and eulogizes the Post-Independence

Indian English poetry. Take for instance, R. Parthasarathy's pronouncement that Indian Verse in English, "did not seriously begin to exist till after the withdrawal of the British from India."[1] P. Lal and Adil Jussawalla are in the company of R. Parthasarathy in denouncing the poetry of Sri Aurobindo and his contemporaries, lock, stock and barrel.

On the other hand, there are critics like K.R.S. Iyengar, V.K. Gokak, C.D. Narasimhaiah and a few others who have lauded the poetry of Sri Aurobindo and his contemporaries like Sarojini Naidu. To Gokak, Sarojini Naidu is the Yeats of India and Sri Aurobindo a great innovator in the art of versification. He classifies the Indian poets in English before Independence into two groups "neo-symbolists" and "neo-modernists". The neo-symbolists dive deep into mysticism and the neo-modernists' vision is coloured by humanism.

C.D. Narasimhaiah speaks of Toru Dutt, Sarojini Naidu and Sri Aurobindo in admiration in his well-known book, *The Swan and the Eagle.* He lauded both Toru and Sarojini as pioneers in the field of Indian English poetry. C.D. Narasimhaiah is more eloquent in his praise of Sri Aurobindo whom he considers not only as a distinguished poet but a critic too. He goes a step forward to tell that English language has gained from Sri Aurobindo and compares him with Joseph Conrad who broadened the descriptive range of the English language. He writes, "It may be said of Sri Aurobindo that he made the English language accommodate certain hitherto unknown (inconscient) areas of experience both through his prose work, 'Life Divine' and through his epic *Savitri,* not to speak of the numerous translations from Sanskrit poetry and drama as well as his other less known but important works."[2] It is interesting and important to remember that Sri Aurobindo nearly succeeded in creating an idiom in English which is peculiar and unique to the genius of Indian people. Well-known scholars and critics like K.R.S. Iyengar, Sisir Kumar Ghose and M.K. Naik too praise Sri Aurobindo and Sarojini Naidu as poets of importance. In the course of an article entitled *Indian Poetry in English—Yesterday-Today-Tomorrow* (*The Literary Criterion* 18:3, 1983:9-18) K.R.S. Iyengar takes R. Parthasarathy, Keki N.

Daruwalla and Adil Jussawalla to task for criticising Sri Aurobindo and earlier poets in English for wrong reasons.

On the other hand, there are sceptics who denounce post-Independence Indian English poets beginning with Nissim Ezekiel. To some Purists, the best post-1947 poets in English would appear as Pseudo-Keats, second-rate Tennyson, third-rate Hardy, and fourth-rate Eliot. It seems to me that a good deal of poetry of our time can be highlighted without denying or denigrating the poetry of our predecessors or taking a parochial and what George Woodcock calls, "literary incestuousness" attitude to recent Indian poetry in English. I believe that serious Indian English poetry came to be written not immediately after Independence but in the Sixties and after. The Indian English poetic movement of the Sixties and Seventies did much to fix its image as deliberately deficient, moderate with a will. Indian English poets sought comparisons with Anglo-Americans and unfortunately, followed either the genteel English poets or the confessing Americans. This tendency has gradually frayed and will probably give way altogether for the fact that however deliberate (and after a faltering start) post-Independence Indian English poetry has proved increasingly robust, varied, responsive to the times and enjoyable. It is now very rarely either consciously indebted or consciously hostile to Anglo-American models, it has acquired a distinct character and discovered its own voice. The voice is discovered by the poet's genius for intimately registering the idiom of his own world.

Post-Independence Indian English poetry is both a break with the past and a continuation with it too. Modernity in recent Indian English poetry, which essentially means a break with the past, has three identifiable manifestations: one—a past-oriented vision which is associated with a sense of loss and hopelessness, a sort of cultural pessimism; two—a future-oriented vision, associated with a desire to remake the world; three—a present-oriented attitude, ahistorical, amoral, neutral, stoic, ironic, ambivalent, absurdist. This modernity has two modes of "expression"—one, it might result in one turning inward going on One's "voyage within"; two, it might result in an ironic observation of reality in "voyage without".

The incipient romanticism and vapid narcissicism of the early Indian English poetry are now discarded in favour of poetry as "a criticism of life". Post-Independence Indian English poetry tries hard to set its roots and develop its own artistic credo. It has successfully risen above "decadent romanticism" and in the hands of such brilliant poets as Nissim Ezikiel, A.K. Ramanujan and R. Parthasarathy, it is acquiring new dimensions.

Jayanta Mahapatra, A.K. Ramanujan, R. Parthasarathy, Arun Kolatkar and Kamala Das turn inward to get into their roots. There is a need to acclimatize English language to an indigenous tradition to write poetry effectively. R. Parthasarathy, as it were, gives a clarion call to Indian English poets to return to their respective linguistic traditions. He asks:

> How long can foreign poets
> Provide the staple of your lines?
> Turn inward, scrape the bottom of your past.
>
> (*Rough Passage*)

It seems natural to conclude that a poet with a live cultural past behind him, aware of his roots and perhaps prejudiced by those roots, has a greater probability of writing significantly than one who has no knowledge of any Indian language other than English. Jayanta Mahapatra's *Relationship* is set in Orissa—a land of "forbidding myth". Mahapatra is "caught in the currents of time" and in his attempt to "go into the unknown in me" tries "to speak of the myth of sleep and action" in order to soothe himself and others who suffer a similar fate. Parthasarathy, Kolatkar and Ramanujan have tried to evoke a sense of their past and inherit the native traditions. Kamala Das too works out her emotional and sexual traumas in poems of unexceptionable frankness reminiscent of the medieval Sahaja poets who espoused free love as a means of realizing oneself. While A.K. Ramanujan's mind seems to be perpetually busy probing the areas of strength and weakness of his Hindu heritage, Kamala Das highlights with boldness the sexual permissiveness and uninhibition rooted in her native culture and produces arresting effect on readers.

Post-Independence Indian English poetry is genuine because it is deeply felt and addressed to the whole community. Indian situation forms a vital part of it. The superstition and folk belief that exist in Indian society, turns out to be a favourite theme of recent poetry. Nissim Ezekiel handles such a theme with superb irony and subdued mockery in *Night of the Scorpion.* The mother is stung, the nationalist and sceptical father tries, "every curse and blessing/ powder, mixture, herb and hybrid," as the peasants swarm to console her, offering advice of a strongly ritualistic and faith healing kind. The mother's reaction to her own suffering, "Thank God, the scorpion picked on me/and spared my children", ironically rejects both the responses. Ramanujan in his much anthologized poem, *A River* does not present the traditional hymns in praise of the river but records instead, the details about the twins, which the women would have borne, bringing the experience to its simple and painful humanity. India's present day ills like brain-drain, too attract the attention of our poets. O.P. Bhatnagar examines the implication of the exodus of the Indian intellectuals to foreign lands and makes a fervent appeal to them to return home. These intellectuals are worse than migrating birds, for the birds, who fly away in winter because of trenchant cold, return home at the turn of the season. But our intellectuals fail to escape the lure of gold and glamour and stay back. Thus, in a poem called *Look Homeward Angel*, Bhatnagar ironically calls them "angels". Likewise, Shiv K. Kumar comes heavily on the politicians who are unprincipled and time-servers. In *Epitaph on an Indian Politician*, Shiv K. Kumar has given a very daring portrayal of the politician:

> Vasectomized of all genital urges
> for love and beauty
> he often crossed floors
> as his wife leaped across beds.

Besides the contemporary problems, there is one vital problem—namely the problem of creating an Indian English idiom which haunts our poets without end. As R. Parthasarathy has rightly observed:

That language is a tree
loses colour
under another sky.

Some of our poets have tried to evoke the sense of "Indianness" both in content and language in their poetry. Ezekiel's "Very Indian Poem in Indian English", "Good-bye Party for Miss Pushpa T.S.", Keki N. Daruwalla's "The Professor Condoles" and R. Parthasarathy's "Incident at Ahmedpore Station" are cases in point.

Nissim Ezekiel, Keki N. Daruwalla, Margaret Chatterjee and Lila Ray, who are unable to share the indigenous tradition take a different attitude, ahistorical, amoral, neutral, stoic and ironic. The expression results in an ironic observation of reality, "Voyage without". O.P. Bhatnagar joins them in making pointed, objective and thought-provoking observations on the reality around us. If poetry written in English in Commonwealth and Third World Countries today is any indication, correctness of language should not be insisted upon. American, Australian, African and West Indian writers have discovered their own idioms in English. Post-Independence Indian English poets have attempted and succeeded to a limited extent in evolving a new Indo-English idiom. Though Indian English poetry has outgrown Victorian taboos and our poets have broken new ground, the quest for cultural moorings seems to be a major preoccupation with them, a trait, they unwittingly share with Madhusudan Dutt, an earlier Indian English poet of repute. But the pervasive presence of this conscious "Indianness" without any trace of romantic nostalgia or exotic quaintness sets contemporary Indian English poetry apart from the imitative mediocrity of much of this poetry in the pre-Independence period.

If as Eliot held, a poem should be able to communicate before it is understood, Mahapatra's poetry has little to fear. What he tries to do is to relate himself to his province (Orissa), and country, its landscape, its history and its milieu. His poetry may not be always simple and sensuous but it is certainly evocative. Contemporary situation, life and living form the bedrock of his poetry. This preoccupation with present day life and society, together with his concern for history, myth and tradition of his country, has taken two modes of expression—one, in turning inward going on one's 'Voyage within', two, turning outward resulting in an ironic observation of reality in 'Voyage without'. In his poetry, one notices a continuous growth and development leading to a higher degree of achievement. He has not looked back since he has published his first book of verse, *Close the Sky Ten by Ten* in 1971. Within the short span of three and a half decades, he has published seventeen volumes of poetry. He now ranks among the best known Third World and Commonwealth poets. His poetry is not only read today but taught as a course in several universities of the world. It has become a topic of M. Phil and Ph.D. dissertations. Jayanta Mahapatra now ranks among the great poets of New Literatures in English in the Third world countries outside the Anglo-American tradition.

## NOTES

1. R. Parthasarathy, (ed) *Ten Twentieth Century Indian Poets* O.U.P. 1976, p. 3.
2. C.D. Narasimhaiah, *The Swan and the Eagle* (Simla: Indian Institute of Advanced Study, 1969), p. 29.

# The Making of the Poet

2

JAYANTA MAHAPATRA is one of the first Indian English Poets to have been honoured both at home and abroad. He is a prolific poet. Though he began writing poetry rather late (he had not published poems before he was forty) he has not looked back since he published his first book of verse, *Close the Sky Ten by Ten* in 1971. His other volumes came in quick succession. *Svaymvara and Other Poems* (1971), *A Father's Hours* (1976), *A Rain of Rites* (1976), *Waiting* (1979), *The False Start* (1980), *Relationship* (1980), *Life Signs* (1983), *Dispossessed Nests* (1986), *Selected Poems* (1987), *Burden of Waves and Fruit* (1988), *Temple* (1989), *A Whiteness of Bone* (1992), *Shadow Space* (1997), *Bare Face* (2000) and *Random Descent* (2005). His poetry shows a continuous development both in theme and technique. Mahapatra is a conscious poet who looks 'before and after' and endlessly revises his poems in order to make them more effective and meaningful.

Jayanta Mahapatra puts down no shutters and puts on no blinkers. He has an open mind and perhaps a willing ear in choosing the themes for his poetry. In his effort to acclimatize English language to an indigenous tradition, Mahapatra has chosen for his theme various subjects beginning from landscape of the country to international problems. A poet's response to the landscape of his country, his sense of tradition and culture of the land of his birth and many other factors go together to make him assume an identity of his own. What Judith Wright observes in this context is very pertinent:

"Before one's country can become an accepted background against which the poet's and novelist's imagination can move unhindered, it must first be observed, understood, described as it were, absorbed. The writer must be at peace with his landscape before he can confidently turn to its human figures."[1]

Jayanta Mahapatra is firmly rooted in the Orissan soil. Puri, Konark, Cuttack, Bhubaneswar form as it were, a quadrangle in the landscape of Mahapatra's poetry. Legends, history and myths associated with these places immensely interest Mahapatra and form the nerve centre of his poetry. He wrote a number of poems on Puri (the great place of Lord Jagannath, the presiding deity of Orissa) one of the four great sacred places of pilgrimage of the Hindus of India.

In these two poems titled 'Dawn at Puri' and 'Main Temple Street, Puri', Mahapatra underlines the importance of Puri and what it means to Hindus in our country. Widows long for breathing their last at Puri lest they should attain salvation. As the poet puts it:

> her last wish to be cremated here
> twisting uncertainly like light
> on the shifting sands. (*Dawn at Puri*)

Since the temple of Lord Jagannath at Puri 'Points to unending rhythm, dying in this place will take one to Silence the ultimate desire of a human being which will enable him to attain 'nirvana'. In another poem titled 'The Temple Road, Puri', Mahapatra describes the 'Stream of common men' on the road to the temple and the form of their prayer. Thus, the poet says,

> Later,
> as the shrine's skeins of light
> slowly close their eyes,
> something reaching into them
> from that place they learn to bear
> the lame lamp post
> to the huge temple door,
> the sacred beads in their hands
> gaping
> at the human ground.
>
> (*The Temple Road, Puri*)

The devotion to the deity makes the devotees humble as they seem to hear his message and begin to understand it. The feeling of universal brotherhood overwhelms them and the heart gets purified. Mahapatra's poetic exploration of the places to which he belongs turns out to be a search for the self. A sense of belonging to the places of his land of birth and to the landscape of his state urges upon the poet to relate it to his poetic craft as is shown in the following lines:

> A man does not mean anything
> But the place
> Sitting on the river bank throwing pebbles
> into the muddy current,
> a man becomes the place.
>
> (*Somewhere, My Man*)

There is as it were, a correspondence between the landscape of a region and the religious faith of the people living there. The landscape of place around the poet is the parameter of his life and faith and perhaps unalterable as his own body. Thus, the landscape is in a way an extension of a person's physical self.

Like Puri, Konark, Bhubaneswar and Cuttack are also important places for Mahapatra as they embody the tradition of ancient Orissa and her heroic past. Poems like 'Indian Summer Poem', 'Evening in an Orissa Village', 'The Orissa Poems', 'The Indian Poems', 'The Indianway' reveal his typical Indian sensibility. Mahapatra has rightly stated his view while receiving the National Akademi of Letters Award in the following words:

'To Orissa, to this land in which my roots lie and lies my past and in which lies my beginning and my end, where the wind knees over the grief of the River Daya and where the waves of Bay of Bengal fail to reach out today to the twilight soul of Konark, I acknowledge my debt and my relationship.'

As V.A. Shahane has observed that 'the main focus of his poetic creativity seems to be centred on the 'naked earth' and the mythological, symbolistic or aesthetic structures firmly rooted in that 'naked earth' of which Orissa and India form a significant part.'[2] The search for roots is a trend in modern Indian English poetry which Mahapatra shares with A.K.

Ramanujan and R. Parthasarathy. Mahapatra's Central Sahitya Akademi Award Winning book, *Relationship* is in a way a quest for Mahapatra's roots. "This poem is no collection of mere observation, a place here, a character there, an unstrenuous meditation or two, inevitable landscapes, but a determined integrated set of selections built into the theme. For the poet, the Orissan landscape is the objective setting of his mental evolution, the phases of which get mixed up with the lyrical vocabulary of a humanist creed. The poem being set in Orissa embodies the myth and history of the land. As the conflicting principles of man and nature, history and autobiography and faith and suffering interact against the vast panorama of Orissan landscape, the poem shows a dialectical progression where every synthesis in further analysis turns into a thesis."[3]

The heroic Oriya past is vividly remembered and recalled with a sense of nostalgia. The glory and pride of our ancestors exhibited in the climactic Kalinga War in 261 B.C. which turned Ashok the Great into a deeply religious man, is now a longlost trait in our racial character. The river Daya is a witness to our ancestor's heroic effort which has become a sort of myth for us. Once heroic and militant race is no more than mere memory now for its successors proved to be unworthy of keeping the glory of their ancestors afloat and drifted away from their ideals. Thus, Mahapatra notices a sharp contrast in the descending order between the past and the present marking an overwhelming decline in values of life in our time. The following passage makes it amply clear:

> It is hard to tell now
> What opened the anxious skies
> how the age old proud stones
> lost their strength and fell
> and how the waters of Daya
> Stank with the bodies of my ancestors
> my eyes close now
> because of the fear that moves my skin.
>
> (*Relationship*)

The poet's life is integrated with the heroic tradition of the land of his birth and as he becomes conscious of it, his heart throbs and a kind of unknown fear engulfs him. The landscape of Orissa moves him when he observes the annual migrating birds from far north Siberia to the warm waters of Chilika, a beautiful lake in Orissa. The agony of the poet springs from the fact that while the birds and animals react naturally to the seasons of the year, he is cut off as it were from the heroic traditions of his ancestors. He tells that 'I can never come alive/ if I refuse to consecrate at the altar of my Origins' and thus 'a prayer to draw my body out of a thousand years'. There is a sense of nostalgia which pervades the atmosphere of the poem. Cuttack, a city of historical importance, which had the great Barabati Fort, is now a symbol of 'vanquished dynasties'. A sense of belonging overwhelms the poet and in a voice charged with emotion he tells us:

> Now I stand among these ruins
> waiting for the cry of a night bird
> from the river's far side
> to drift through my weariness
> listening to the voices of my friends
> who have become the friends of others
> writing poems, object and anxious
> in rooms which reek of old folk,
> of their sloth and arthritis and neglect,
> like state cupboards which are going black
> with the smells of the rancid fat of the past.
>
> (*Relationship*)

There seems to be a need for pilgrimage to the 'Living Oriya Past' in order to recognize the present and lead a meaningful life by imbibing spirit of the glorious past and tradition of the land. Mahapatra underlines this aspect emphatically in course of an article in *The Literary Criterion:*

"*Relationship* is a product of dreams, has made me speak of the demands of a pilgrimage—a pilgrimage threatened by the living Oriya past, by nagging hunger and a persistent sexuality."[4]

If this long poem 'Relationship' is an amalgam of history, myth and vision, there are quite a few poems in which the poet turns to his private history like his own family to make an inward journey to establish his link with the past. It is in this aspect, he resembles three outstanding contemporary Indian English poets namely A.K. Ramanujan, R. Parthasarathy and Kamala Das. Like Kamala Das's grandmother, Jayanta Mahapatra's grandfather is a dominant figure in his family poems. In a poem called 'Grandfather', Mahapatra dives deep into his family history and reflects the basic issues of life including change of religion. Driven by hunger, the poet's grandfather, Chintamani Mahapatra embraced Christianity during the devastating famine that struck Orissa in 1866. With a sense of agony and disgust, the poet directs his volley of questions to his grandfather, only to regret it in the end. Thus, the past comes alive for a moment to remind us of the misfortune that befell on our people to choose the path they did. We may now 'Change and smile but the agony abides'. The poet rightly asks:

> What did faith matter?
> What Hindu World so ancient and true for you to hold?

When we analyse the consequences of that great famine, our conscience pricks us. What remains between our ancestors and us is 'a conscience of years'. The poet rightly feels that it is no use to hold our ancestors responsible for the change of faith and regrets:

> We wish we knew you more,
> we wish we knew what it was to be, against dying,
> to know the dignity.
>
> (*Grandfather*)

In another poem called 'The Hour Before Dawn', the poet records his concern for his ailing father. The poem is imbued with a sense of pathos when the poet apprehends his father's death:

> My father, sad-faced father (How very far you are
> from this empty room filled only with myself!)
> without a sound the dark tree out there

struggles with its death in my life.
The silent world floats beside me;
tomorrow may be I'll hear my father is dead
but he might bear the face of my son.

(*The Hour Before Dawn*)

This is a significant poem for it embodies the Hindu faith that parents are born to their children as their children, which Mahapatra shares with other Indians. This prompts the poet to look within and to know his own self. As he puts it:

This evening I look at that part of myself
which remains with me, but I do not know
what it is, hard to recognize it anymore.

(*Of This Evening*)

In some of Mahapatra's poems; Indian landscape, seasons and environment become the starting point of giving his imagination a freeplay to reflect on his private moments of desire, despair, guilt and illumination. The poems which belong to this category are 'Dawn', 'Village', 'Oldplaces', 'Summer', 'A Twilight Poem', 'Appearance', 'Silence', 'Indian Summer Poem', 'Evening', 'Evening Landscape by the River', 'The Captive Air of Chandipur-on-Sea', 'A Country', 'An October Morning', 'The Wind', and a few others. The landscape often reminds the poet of our past glory and the dead who had once inhabited the place. Thus, the poet writes:

The cries of fishermen come drifting through the spray,
music of what the world has lost.

(*The Captive Air of Chandipur-on-Sea*)

This is the kind of sadness which closed the eyes.
Here the memory for faces of the dead never appears.

(*Evening Landscape by the River*)

In both these poems, the past is recalled through fishermen who are lively characters in Mahapatra's poetry. Landscape is vital to the understanding of his poetry, for it enables Mahapatra to portray the inner reality by making allusion to it. Reality when apprehended through the landscape not only becomes gloomy but poignant which moves us. As the poet puts it:

Sometimes at night when all voices die
My mind sees the earth, my country
to accept sacrifice..................................
..............................................................
wherever I try to live,
in pious pretence at Puri
or in the fiery violence of a revolutionary
my reason becomes a prejudiced sorrow
like socialism.
And not understanding myself,
not understanding you,
like the still strange shapes of hills in the distance,
I too, listen to the far away wailing of hyenas
aware of the dying countryside around them,
tortured by hunger and the reek of decay in the air
after the age-old myths have been told all over again.

(*A Country*)

Thus, landscape has a great significance in Mahapatra'a poetry so far as it enables the poet to search for his own self in order to understand the world in its proper perspective. The landscape also helps the poet to alleviate his suffering.

I would forget the causes of suffering, mine and others,
to justify my evening's spirit, searching the landscape
for the leafs green, the stone's ochre,
for what I would not make of myself.

(*Evening*)

Sun and moon, dawn and dusk, day and night, heat and dust, mountains and sea, river and hills, sky and earth all are incorporated into the texture of his landscape poetry in his effort to depict the predicament of modernman in an irreligious milieu. He is not a romantic poet to sing songs in praise of the beauty of nature. He is a realist who sees life against the backdrop of landscape but does not run away. He sees life in life's terms and, therefore, a calm serenity governs his landscape poems. Landscape poems such as 'An Evening by the River', 'Of a Dawn', 'A Time', 'An October Morning', and 'The Wind' are included in his eleventh volume of poems called *Burden of Waves* and *Fruit* (1988). These poems are burdened with a consciousness that makes him 'see into the life of things'. As the poet observes:

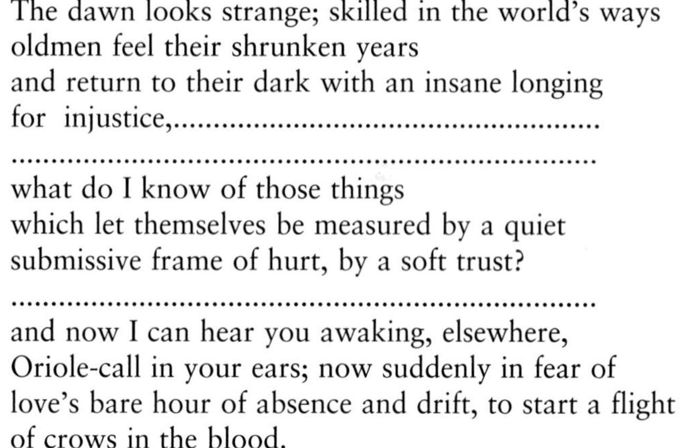

> The dawn looks strange; skilled in the world's ways
> oldmen feel their shrunken years
> and return to their dark with an insane longing
> for injustice,.....................................................
> ..........................................................................
> what do I know of those things
> which let themselves be measured by a quiet
> submissive frame of hurt, by a soft trust?
> ..........................................................................
> and now I can hear you awaking, elsewhere,
> Oriole-call in your ears; now suddenly in fear of
> love's bare hour of absence and drift, to start a flight
> of crows in the blood.

(*Of a Dawn*)

Unlike Wordsworth, Mahapatra does not view nature uncritically. In a poem called, 'Story at the Start of 1978' records how life and property have been lost or damaged due to the great cyclone that lashed the Andhra and Orissa coast in 1978 and left behind a great destruction unsurpassed in recent history. Mahapatra, in the words of V.A. Shahane, 'invokes with vivid detail the atmosphere of that savage storm, the wind plucking the jasmines with its fierce and destructive darkness, the palm leaves screening the epics in their sleep, the wind with its horrible speed causing grave havoc, the storm as the great killer of men and animals."[5]

Landscape has sharpened Mahapatra's sensitivity and he has devoted a full book, *Dispossessed Nests* to the hard realities that one encounters in our country in the present time. In an introduction to this book, the editors note:

"In *Dispossessed Nests*, one hears these wails of a world shattered within a human heart. Like burning rods of truth Mahapatra's poems branded the Screens of our consciousness. In these poems we find deeply anguished outpours of an acutely sensitive man aspiring to capture a disintegrated world in the light of metaphors deriving their heat either from the torturous memory of the country's recent past or from a minute observation of the natural components."[6]

In the 1980s things have taken a turn for the worse so far as law and order is concerned. The anti-national activities in Punjab in the name of Khalistan and the Bhopal Gas tragedy have sent shock waves throughout the country. The blurb of the book rightly makes a note of it in the following words:

"Mahapatra unleashes the buried horror of long and Supreme knives in Punjab and the barbarous dance of bejewelled snakes, of multinational companies in Bhopal. The poems are bitter experiences of the Indian masses betrayed by an inhuman set-up."[7]

Bloodshed, violence and destruction have become the hallmark of today's world. Death is the all pervasive force in *Dispossessed Nests*. Death is the only thing that lasts. Compared to the troubled State of Punjab all other States are by and large peaceful. The poet minutely observes it with a sense of fear and disappointment.

Thus, the poet observes:

In these parts down south
we say we are calm people
who go to sleep without misgivings
we never take our lives seriously
Or perhaps
we don't let ourselves get carried away.
But somewhere
amidst bewildered wheat fields
the cool night wind snips off the skin
from the firm fruit of reason.

(*Dispossessed Nests*, p. 15)

Indiscriminate killings have caused panic all over the country and the situation reminds us of W.B. Yeats's *The Second Coming* where 'things fall apart: the centre cannot hold/mere anarchy is loosed upon the world'. Again we are reminded of the macabre images in the Jacobean tragedy when heads are chopped off and people are strangled mercilessly. Mahapatra describes one such scene in the following lines:

Around
a slender waist
a petticoat stirs
in the wind,
looking absurd
the torso
looking about
for its missing head.

(*Dispossessed Nests*, p. 18)

Humanity has lost its way into oblivion and hate reigns supreme. Man has degraded himself to the level of animals and 'jungle law' prevails. In these circumstances, it is difficult to find a way out as things drift apart with the passing of each day. Thus, the poet writes:

Here
I do not know
what I am looking for.

(*Dispossessed Nests*, p. 20)

Hoping against hope the poet wonders if 'this is the last explosion'. The senseless violence has robbed off man of his conscience and as the poet puts it ironically:

Now a man knows only two ways
for dealing with a stray woman:
he rapes her
and he kills her

(*Dispossessed Nests*, p. 33)

Mahapatra depicts the horror of life due to violent Khalistan movement and Bhopal Gas tragedy in all its details. With a tone deeply imbued with pathos, the poet observes that 'the country we try to leave behind seems upset by its own silence' and people smell the danger that awaits them in future. Life has lost its charm as it is beset with danger and uncertainty. Thus, the poet writes:

I can hear the broken voice of the night,
Crying in my hands, bloody and black,
and carrying with it the Joint Smells
of flowers well past their best

(*Dispossessed Nests*, p. 49)

If the happenings in Punjab and the Gas Tragedy in Bhopal make the poet sad, the brute massacre at Nellie in Assam breaks his heart. Violence anywhere is reprehensible for the poet. When the world around us seems to be out of tune, when purblindmen enact hell, when good intentions fatally miscarry, can poetry save us? That's a million dollar question. Mahapatra tries to answer this question in his own way.

> But what use is a poem, once writing is done?
> Words looking for what, in the dark of the soul?
> like the sound of a match striking, then over,
> I know that much. When all else has failed,
> the poem's words are perhaps justified.
>
> (*Last Night the Poem*)

This takes us to another poem titled, "Will a poem of mine be the only answer?" in which the poet states that a special kind of feeling he gets from his poems though they do not solve all problems. The world would have been an illusion to him without his poems.

Love as a theme dwindles at the hands of Mahapatra. He examines it from various angles but it remains largely unfulfilled. That is the reason why he talks of love and sex freely. Some of his important love poems are 'Another Evening', 'Women in Love', 'The Whorehouse in a Calcutta Street', 'Hunger', 'Armour', 'Love Fragment', 'Of That Love', 'Lost', and a few others. The past is recalled in nostalgia. As Mahapatra puts it:

> of that love, of that mile
> walked together in the rain,
> only a weariness remains ..............
> .............. Years have passed
> Since I sat with you, watching
> the sky grow lonelier with cloudlessness
> waiting for your body to make it lived in.

In 'Lost' the poet recalls the lost woman whom he made love and the past is brought back alive as he watched the changing contours of her body. In 'Another Evening' the longing for his beloved whom he has lost, overwhelms the protagonist and hence the lamentation.

Your absence
is part of growing older, and this October
a time for measuring an indefatigable memory.

(*Another Evening*)

'Women in Love' expresses poet's passion for love. Even after consummation of love, the poet asks for a sort of permanent union with God.

Women, what things
you would make me remember
what would you make me do.

(*Women in Love*)

Love in Mahapatra's poetry remains largely unrequitted and, therefore, he suggests the need for consummation in love through subtle images. He talks of love and sex freely in an effort to get over disappointments and failures in love life. In a poem titled 'Hunger' Mahapatra depicts a scene in which a fisherman in order to satisfy his hunger invites a stranger to enjoy his fifteen year old daughter. The word 'hunger' is both literal and symbolic for it also refers to sex starvation. The protagonist recalls the incident in the following words:

I heard him say: my daughter, she's just turned
fifteen ....
Feel her, I'll be back soon, your bus leaves at nine.
The sky fell on me and a father's exhausted wile.
Long and lean, her years were cold as rubber.
She opened her wormy legs wide. I felt the hunger
there,
the other one, the fish slithering turning inside.

(*Hunger*)

The coveted sexual imagery suggesting the consummation in a subtle way. In another poem called 'Of Armour' the secret physical union is shown in a more controlled way without stating things in an open manner. As the poet puts it:

She is where you have followed her
and where her fleating panting space
covers up your declivitous time

For it seemed to be a time
when waters flow past without their purposes,
when replicas of temples lie scattered everywhere
..............................................
and if it was the time, I thought
to be conquered by a sleep that had come to rest
On the unmoving dreams of our past

(*Relationship*)

Like Eliot, Mahapatra believes in the paradox that time can be conquered only through time.

When one scans the whole range of Mahapatra's poetry, one notices a wider variety of themes covering a large number of subjects. Love, death, tradition, rituals and contemporary reality all attract him and he has taken all these as themes. But what gives an identity to his poetry is the breadth of his understanding, the temper of his mind and the depth of his vision. He sees life 'steadily and sees it whole'. His characters particularly in *Relationship* and *Temple* are recognisable in terms of their chief intensity and therefore they appeal to us in our own situation. It will not be wholly accurate to judge Mahapatra's poetry as a product of the 'modernist movement' of the first half of our century, as Bruce King does because the entire corpus of his poetry defies such an estimation. His poetic persona is not 'half guessed' and 'half-understood' and not always a shadowy figure. On the other hand, I see a clear development in the poetry of Mahapatra beginning with *Rain of Rites* and culminating in *Relationship*. Even after *Relationship* there is no denouement and his poesy continues to fly in its wings as high as ever.

*Life Signs, Dispossessed Nests, Burdens of Waves and Fruit*, *Temple*, and *A Whiteness of Bone* do not show any sign of decline in his poetic calibre and Mahapatra continues to be where he was with the crowning of his achievement in *Relationship* in 1980, Mahapatra's variety, continuity and achievement remain unsurpassed in contemporary Indian English poetry and as such he has few peers and not many equals among recent Indian English poets.

of his being, which the writer exploits in symbols of his own making'.

The 'Time' theme makes an interesting reading in Mahapatra's poetry. Here he seems to have been influenced by T.S. Eliot. He does not believe in linear development of time when time passes like an arrow in the direction of past, present and future. Instead, he believes in the circular motion of time where present becomes the focal point of past, present and future. P.C. David has rightly pointed out that "Mahapatra presents time choosing today as the focal point of time and also as a repository of past, present and future. The poem is characteristically entitled 'Today' in which he brings all the experiences of the past years to concentrate on one day and then prospects the future through today."[8]

Here are a few examples from Mahapatra's poetry:

Time faces me and there
like the lucking madness in a tyrant's eye
is the whom of another day
dark wings shut and unmoving in the blue.
This day is an instant which possesses me
from which I cannot escape

(*Today*)

Time is also viewed as a part of eternity in the following lines:

Here is the stone, the taste
of the poison in the lungs,
the broad polished gestures that say
the world will not come to an end

(*Through the Stone*)

But time has no mouth
and the black labyrinth
of casuarinas along the edges of the sea
closes the sky's eternal vault ...............

Now caught in the currents of time
I watch the blue of the sky
Seep out slowly

(*Relationship 1*)

'The Lost Children of America' is a well-known poem which depicts the predicament of young American people who come here in search of peace and solace and wander their way into oblivion. Here in our country we are not the angels of morality and virtue as we were thought to be. The poet probes into the heart of these youngmen and women of America who come to our country and regret that we are no better than them to show them the way. The reality is felt in the pulses and may be along the heart as the poet describes the wandering youngmen and women of America. Thus, the poet writes:

> they wander, these lost children of America
> fluenting their long unkempt hair and bare feet,
> a man naked to the waist, the fringes
> of his torm shorts two weary chapped mouths —
> a woman, her face of old porcelain
> burnt in the harsh sun
> clothed indifferent in a discoloured sack
> her breasts weak and sagging
> having lost their glimmer and their power
> these lost children wonder bare-eyed
> Smelling of incense and living on grass and flowers
> like scavengers accompanied by their impressive shadows
> Perhaps in search of many gods, to ask for strength
> with their appearance of sibyls and witches
> limp and cold with ablutions
> of another, separate world.
> We gaze at each other in silence, the lost child and
> Who knows who is playing a joke on whom?
>
> (*The Lost Children of America*)

Against the backdrop of this international youth unrest is shown the hypocrisy of our own generation giving a lie to our tradition of being a moral conscious nation. Contemporary reality not only appeals to the poet but it also helps him to describe life as he sees it. Life is portrayed as it is rather than as it should have been. In course of an article contributed to *The Literary Criterion*, Mahapatra makes it clear that the 'experiences at various times in the writer's life have clothed the assentiality

Rain stands on the margins of my time,
a discovery, like theft,
making me careful how I lay the hour down,
looking at the trees growing too large
for my little yard, filling with lurid light,
and I hardly see spring coming in.
(*Again the Rain Falls*)

Apart from evoking traditional themes and making an indigenous tradition available in English, Mahapatra also writes on contemporary situation and problems that one encounters in our day to day life. Poems like 'A Monsoon Day Fable' and 'The Lost Children of America' are cases in point. A personal failure leads the poet to see the failure in all fronts in national as well as intellectual arena which makes him realise the futility of human relationship. The Monsoon which makes him nostalgic about the past and brings before his mind's eye the 'ageing dancer' whom he admired shocks him with the sight of cows taken towards the municipal slaughter house to be butchered. Not only that, the empty rhetoric of the politicians and the artificiality of our poets also make us feel ashamed of our hypocritical existence. Everything seems to be out of tune when no law works—thanks to our selfishness. Thus, the poet says,

The Cuttack dawn herds the emaciated cows
toward the municipal slaughter house, their feet
slipping, their eyes following the vague light
into silence. Wet as though with glue, they haunt
me through the nights, perhaps equipped with designs
to show man his true nature.........
I pick up the morning newspaper and see
how a nation goes on insulting itself
with its own web of rhetoric. And remember how
some of us poets had participated at the Silver Jubilee
Celebrations of the Sahitya Akademi in New Delhi
and with plagiarized smiles and abstract talk convinced
ourselves that in harmony there was no deception.
(*A Monsoon Day Fable*)

The monsoon reminds the poet of our loveless lives that seem to be out of tune in our society and everyday existence.

## NOTES

1. Quoted by Devindra Kohli, "Landscape and Poetry" *The Journal of Commonwealth Literature,* 13 : 3, April 1979 : 54.
2. V.A. Shahane, "The Naked Earth and Beyond: The Poetry of Jayanta Mahapatra", *Perspectives on Indian Poetry in English* (New Delhi: Abhinav Publication 1984) : 144.
3. Bijay Kumar Das, *Critical Perspectives on 'Relationship' and 'Latter-day Psalms'* (Bareilly: PBD, 1986) : 40.
4. Jayanta Mahapatra, 'The Inaudible Resonance in English Poetry in India,' *The Literary Criterion* 15 : 1 1980 : 36.
5. V.A. Shahane, "The Naked Earth and Beyond: The Poetry of Jayanta Mahapatra", *Perspectives on Indian Poetry in English*: 149.
6. (Ed.) Yayatsa R.D. and Ramanand Rathi, *Dispossessed Nests* (Introduction) (Jaipur: Nirala Publication) 1986 : 10.
7. *Ibid.* (Blurb of the book).
8. P.C. David, 'The Concept of Time in the False Start', *The Poetry of Jayanta Mahapatra, A Critical Study* (New Delhi: Sterling Publishers Pvt. Ltd.) 1986 : 252.

# The Development of Technique

# 3

WE no longer value poetry for its content only. Form is as important as content and it greatly contributes to the techinque of the poem and enriches its meaning. The contemporary poet encounters a complex world and his poetry is an outcome of his interaction with such a world. Hence his poetry has become difficult, complex, obscure and allusive. Jayanta Mahapatra is no exception. He explains his position in a straightforward manner and underlines the value of symbols and images in his poetry:

"Today's poem utilizes a number of images and symbols to form a whole, leaving the reader to extricate himself with the valid meaning or argument from them ... This is true of much of the poetry I have written."[1] He further states that 'a seemingly obscure poem does in its content, contain the hidden voice for its ultimate understanding'.[2] His argument gains ground when he says that, if contemporary life is no longer what it was, say twenty-five years back, can one expect the same content, the same form, the same substance from contemporary poems?[3] He also agrees with the point of view that 'a great poem lets us embark on a sort of journey or voyage through symbols and allusions to encompass the human condition'.[4]

It is clear from the lines quoted above "that Mahapatra lays emphasis on the technique of the poem and takes care of imagery and symbols in his poetry. He believes that, "the capacity or power of conducting the essential experience of the poem will primarily depend upon the poem itself—on the poem's design."[5] He seems to have been influenced by the imagist movement and particularly by Eliot and Ezra Pound to lay emphasis on the images of the poem. He states his position very clearly in the following lines:

"Perhaps I begin with an image or a cluster of images or an image leads to another, or perhaps the images belonging to a sort of 'group'.... The image starts the movement of the poem...but I do not know where I am proceeding in the poem or how the poem is going to end. It is as though I am entering a region of darkness, a place of the mind which I have never visited before. Or if I have visited it, I have not been able to see into all the corners of that place. Therefore, without conscious reasoning, I grope from one level to another in my mind and try to reach the end. That's how the end of a poem of mine comes about, and it is exploratory, no doubt, because I don't know myself how the poem is going to be."[6]

As a significant poet rooted in the traditions of Orissa, Mahapatra makes use of religious imagery and symbols in his poetry. He has acknowledged that, 'the entire land literally spills with ancient temples and their ruins... and Puri continues to be the hub of Orissa's cultural-religious life, around the great Temple of Jagannath.'[7] His own reaction to the Puri temples is as follows:

"You seem somewhat afraid to be there, yet one time or another something drags you there without your knowing. All the time you feel it, heart pounding on, beyond you, in the immediate darkness—not beating for its own, but for those millions who came here every year, once at least before their present lives end.... It's (the Great Temple's) immensity is surprisingly tender; I experience the touch of a huge hand beneath me, through my skin. I cannot explain it."[8] This makes Mahapatra's use of religious imagery clear. Mahapatra's poetry is significant because of the symbols, myths and imagery which make it different from the poetry of other contemporary poets. 'Rain' for example, is a recurrent symbol in Mahapatra's poetry. K. Ayyappa Paniker underlines the importance of the rain symbol in the following words:

In Mahapatra's 'Scheme of Sin and Expiation', it is rain that seems to work out the hope for expiation. The process of purification is also a rain of rites.[9]

The title poem in 'A Rain of Rites' contains the question, "what holds my rain so it's hard to overcome?" This immediately reminds us of the tradition which binds the poet with his past. Rain here a symbol of wisdom is an eye opener for us to apprehend reality. It evokes our memory (racial memory) and symbolizes the primordial innocence of man. Rain is an all pervasive metaphor in Mahapatra's poetry. It not only links man with the universe as a symbol of fertility, it also evokes his past and reminds him of the suffering he had undergone in life. Thus, the poet writes:

> The rain I have known and traded all this life
> is thrown like kelp on the beach.
>
> (*A Rain of Rites*)

This rain has an impact on the minds of people. It evokes both the memory and the desire and therefore represents both past and future. Since both past and future, paradoxically meet in the present, the rain also represents the present. As Mahapatra rightly says,

> I see
> it play over people, piled up to their silences
> It creates an impression of vastness
> It quietly opens a door.
>
> (*A Rain*)

In the words of V.A. Shahane, "*Rain*, for Mahapatra, is thus both a ritual and reality—ritual of purifying oneself as well as the reality of seasons, the cyclical change in the Indian year, in Orissa's wet and fertile landscape—the naked earth covered by the waters of the Mahanadi and its tributaries which in fact, surround the town of Cuttack from three sides making it virtually an island."[10]

Rain is an all pervasive symbol—both creative and destructive in Mahapatra's poetry. 'A rain that does not wet the earth any more/lost of purpose, like a benediction', 'where day breaks fat and treacherous with rain' reveal the destructive nature of rain. Rain is also evocative of one's memory and hence it helps a person to hark back to the past. Here are a few examples.

All night I have waited for the rain to end,
the forbidden memories ringing, compelling
footfalls among the ruins, the day's last sun—smoking
in unending fields soaked in innocence.

(*Four Rain Poems*)

Once again, it has been a day of rain
And I hear the flutter of light feet
On the warm earth, excited wings
loosening from the dark.

Or what habit palpitates
inside the dark pit of love:
art, ceremony or voice that lies
under my aimless hearing of rain?

(*A Day of Rain*)

Rain stands on the margins of my time
a discovery, like theft.
making me careful how I lay the hour down.

(*Again the Rain Falls*)

There is also another aspect of this symbol of 'rain' which is positive and welcome. In a poem called 'Rains in Orissa' the poet describes the rainy season in Orissa, his home State, in an artistic manner. Thus, he writes:

The sky's face expressionless.
An oriole call echoes away in the sullen grayness,
the book of earth throbs with the light of things
A pond heron floats wearily in a rainpool.
Its face a mask, it pauses for another look around.
Grass everywhere is huge and moves forward to kill.

(*Rains in Orissa*)

The landscape of Orissa in rainy season comes alive here. This rain is also evocative of sexual passion and desire. Mahapatra here seems to have been influenced by our ancient Sanskrit as well as Oriya poets to take 'rain' as a catalyst of fuelling sexual passion. Thus, he says:

Rain that falls silently in a July sky
catching in your trembling skin

pearls of fire,
... ... ...
who can bear the thought
of his woman going out with someone else
rain falling on with frightened eyes
clay that bites the one
who gave it life.

(*The Rain Falling*)

'Rain' for Mahapatra is not only a symbol but it is a metaphor of life. He loves it as he loves his own life and, therefore, he cannot live without. Thus, very appropriately he states:

In the end
I come back to the day and to the rain

(*In the Fields of Desolate Rice*)

'Rain' being a regenerative symbol recurs frequently in a number of poems. Thus, the poet says,

It has been raining again
and the water drips upon the bones,
flowing into the cold earth where
the dead lie easily in rows.
This is the time when the poem
raises itself once again, unknown wings
brushing the face of darkness of our loving
to make us ask: Does one find death
in an act which comes out of love?

'Rain', an old symbol in our ancient literatures stands for fertility, life and sometimes for separation in Mahapatra's poetry. This seems to be the most favourite symbol of Mahapatra. Images play a vital role in Mahapatra's poetry. His images are subtle, controlled, apt and moving. They heighten the significance of the meaning of the poems by hinting at it in a cool and ordered manner. Take for instance, the protagonist's sex experience with a teen-aged daughter of a fisherman has been conveyed to us through an astonishingly compact image, 'the fish silthering turning inside'. I am inclined to agree with S.K. Desai when he says,

"The falling of the father's will and the tremendous falling of the sky lead the reader onto the sexual fall of the protagonist —the 'fall' being both literal and metaphorical. The sex experience in the context is 'cold as rubber', the coldness and the deadness suggesting further an association of death and the grave in the words, her wormy legs." The protagonist finally feels the hunger there, 'the other one' not the sexual hunger but the one in the stomach. The final image unifies a stunningly imaginative vision all the strands implicit in the poem; the fisherman returning with his catch, his catching of the youngman; the youngman's confused agitation; the unsatisfactory elusive sex experience—the entire situation in which everybody is a suffering victim."[11]

The shadows of W.B. Yeats and T.S. Eliot loom large in *Relationship*. Images of sleep, twilight, phantom darkness, half light of rain, the pallor of dreams, the granite eyes are needed to see the stones throb, remind of Eliot's imagery in *The Hollowmen*. Yeats's 'Sailing to Byzantium' influences Mahapatra's imagery in 'Relationship'. Imagery in section V and IX of *Relationship* has been influenced by W.B. Yeats's "Sailing to Byzantium". Take for instance, the image of 'the strange country in which you weave your flaming play' in section V, which is clearly influenced by Yeats's beginning, 'That is no country for old men. The young/in one another's arms....' Again 'the supple figures' multiplying 'their mute echoes of another fire on stone' are like Yeats's 'the artifice of eternity'. 'Fire' and 'Pyre' are reminiscent of 'fire', 'gyre' and 'desire' in Yeats's poem. Moreover, 'the special vision/of our poignant significance' sounds like Yeats's 'Studying/Monuments of its own Magnificance'.

Regarding Eliot's influence Ajit Khullar makes an apt observation:

"Mahapatra has taken Eliot in his stride and reduced his voice to one among many that 'go in and out of the city gates' of *Relationship*. When one reads of 'this brassy October afternoon' Eliot's' 'April is the cruellest month' starts vying for attention. Eliot's influence pervades Mahapatra's lines about 'loneliness' on an October afternoon when he sees 'the secret coves on the naked beach/charred by old fires and littered with picnic paper and empty bottles'. Such images as 'a galvanometer needle/ between the zero and the hundred of gloom' and 'shameless fevers whose viruses tear the skin like paper' are all Eliotian.[12]

Apart from Yeats and Eliot, Mahapatra is also influenced by Whitman's imagery. Image like 'hawk-like calmy circling overhead' bring to mind Whitman's image of the spotted hawk that 'Swops by' in *Song of Myself* (Section 52). Imagery plays a vital role in conveying the contour of love in Mahapatra's poetry. The images are highly evocative in their context and Mahapatra hints at the consummation of love or lack of it with the subtle touch of an artist without making it overt and plain. For instance, when teen-aged school girls witness a bull and a cow copulating in the street under the supervision of elders, on their way to school, they feel the subtle touch of love in the dark corners of their heart. Thus, the poet says,

> ... two shy twelve year olds
> glance surreptitiously, then turn their heads away.
> It is only human mirrors which shape
> an embarrassed scene. Their own hushed bodies
> amaze them. Lost in respectability's ruse,
> they stare at the road, learning to close their eyes,
> to hold their keen pride.
>
> (*Sunburst*)

In another poem called 'Hunger' the poet hints at the fulfilment of lust in a very subtle way when the protagonist at the suggestion of the fisherman defiles the body of his fifteen year old daughter. Hunger and lust degenerated both the primitive and the sophisticated and brought the beast in them into open. As the poet puts it:

> It was heard to believe the flesh was heavy on my back.
> The fisherman said: Will you have her, carelessly...
> I heard him say: My daughter, she's just turned fifteen
> Feel her, I'll be back soon, your bus leaves at nine
> The sky fell on me, and a father's exhausted will
> Long and lean, her years were cold as rubber
> she opened her wormy legs wide. I felt the hunger there,
> the other one, the fish slithering, turning inside.

The image of fish as the male organ of sex is very appropriate here, particularly when the daughter belongs to a fisherman and fishing is the profession. Hence, both the profession and prostitution join in her in a bid to unite hunger and lust. The irony is implicit in the context.

The consummation of love follows marriage in the Indian context but that does not foreclose the meetings of lovers before it. 'Rain' being the initiator of love which fuels the desire and the lovers burn inside though they keep the outward calm. The lover counsels prudence though he likes her to be very close to him. The marriage is awaited. Thus, the poet describes:

> We would return again and again
> to the movement
> that is neither forward nor backward,
> and let the sun and moon take over,
> trailing their substances and shadows.
>
> you know
> I could not touch you
> like that,
> until our wedding night.
>
> (*The Indian Way*)

The echo of Eliot is distinct and unmistakable.

In 'Woman in Love', a woman's body is likened to the blue waves of the sea and the lover to a boat which drifts apart in the blue waves, while the woman's soul is continuous like the tide unaware of the drifting of the boat. The image suggests that a woman is vast like the waves and the lover like a boat is unable to measure her depth. This is a new thought provoking image. Symbols play a vital role in enriching Mahapatra's poetry. Circle, Sky, Dawn, Sun, Moon and Rain are recurrent symbols in his poetry. Eliot seems to have influenced Mahapatra in choosing some of his symbols like circle and sky. Sun is one of the earliest symbols used in his early volume of poems like 'A Father's Hours'. Moon, for Mahapatra is an antithetical symbol of the sun and it symbolizes for him a sense of shattered dreams. Thus, he writes:

> Later, the moon would rise, blood red,
> Lighting the soul's edge like a flame.
>
> (*The Storm*)

The Moon is also evocative of the past. When the starlight 'rolls restlessly on the mat, there is the moon that is taking me somewhere', says the poet. The Moon is also symbolic of the poet's 'buried self' that hides the secret of his life. Thus, the poet asks:

> What humility is that which will not let me reveal the real?
> What shameful secret lies hidden in the shadows of my
> moon?
>
> (*The Moon Moments*)

Most of Mahapatra's symbols are personal symbols used for specific purposes. They are not static symbols like that of Eliot. On the other hand, they are dynamic and keep on changing their meanings like the personal symbols of W.B. Yeats. If Eliot says he could 'Connect nothing with nothing', Mahapatra states that, 'we drag meanings from what we see'. It is in this context his poems assume a greater significance and hence the justification of symbols. Symbols and myths play a vital role in Mahapatra's poetry particularly when he tries to come to terms with Hindu mythology. Mahapatra seems to believe in the Hindu belief that the Universe is boundless and everything occurs simultaneously and all possibilities may exist without excluding each other. Regarding the idea of opposites, Mahapatra writes:

"So, poetry, poetry that has been Indian in essence, does take us beyond ourselves, bringing us face to face with the self on the other side, revealing suddenly the mirror opposite the idea that has gone to make the poem. Once again, this is a coming together of opposites—like, for instance, good and evil, which can only carry themselves as ideas or exist because one has meaning only in relation to another. One could go on to cite examples from the domain of science, to show that such existence is a reality in the world of subatomic particle—the electron which has its opposite in the position, for instance—and such pairs of eternal antipodes in the minutest forms of matter. And so it is, perhaps with poetry. If an idea is there, it must exist as a pair of opposites; if you have one, you must have the other, because one has meaning in relation to the other. And the human mind can only think in terms of these possibilities."[13]

In a poem called 'Ikons' he gives vent to these contrary impulses:

Black ikons:
a museum of symbols
silence the land...
Among them a father stands,
looking around, like a hill.
Then mumbling to himself,
he touches the linga with his forehead,
divine earths closing his eyes, a sightless—god,
his charred silence
left from an enormous fire
no one can remember.

"Ikons": The 'Linga' is the phallic symbol of black, polished stone, it is the object of worship in temples dedicated to Siva, the Destroyer, the most powerful god of the Hindu trinity. Frank Allen makes an interesting comment on this poem:

"I see the man's pain not as frustrated energy, as though he were a Tennessee Williams unfrocked cleric but colliding impulses allowed a maximum assertion. He must communicate with a remorseless blind phallic earth while 'a museum of symbols' silences the land. An unself-conscious recognition of rhythms of the 'lingam' and 'yoni' (Symbols of male and female genitals) animate and free the best of these poems, like 'The Whorehouse in a Calcutta Street' and 'Hunger' from stridency. If their imaginative exploration of the sexual dimension of the psyche remains perturbed and opaque, they do not at least cry out ingenuously for false heavens and false hells. The god of the lingam from antiquity has been Siva, the destroyer, simultaneously 'auspicious' god of ascetics, because sexual energy, to the Hindu, is ultimately radiant spiritual energy.'[14]

The same symbol of procreation is used in the eighth section of *Relationship* in a bid to recreate a new world order. This is how the section ends:

For now I touch your secret order,
embarrassed 'Yoni',
before me lie the sulking years of dreams,

him, confined his cousin and her husband in prison and killed all their offspring as soon as they were born. But Krishna, the eighth child, was smuggled out of prison and taken to live with his foster parents elsewhere. Kamsa ordered the ogress Putana to kill all the boys born in his kingdom during the month in which his cousin had expected the birth of her child, because he was unaware of her whereabouts. Putana, transformed into a beautiful woman, with a deadly poison smeared over her nipples, finally arrived at the house where the child-Krishna lived. There she took Krishna from his foster mother's arms with a show of maternal love and gave him her poisoned breasts to suckle. Krishna sucked so hard that he not only drank all Putana's milk but he sucked her life away. The ogress swooned, with Krishna's mouth at her breast. As she fell dead she regained her original hideous form. The legend concludes that Putana nevertheless attained moksha since she had acted as mother, even though an evil one, to the child-God."[16]

There is a mistake in the note to the Putana myth—that is, Lord Krishna is the son of Kamsa's sister—not his cousin as stated. Mahapatra uses the myth of 'Laxmanrekha' in *Temple* to show the limits beyond which one should not go lest the devil should take her. In the *Ramayan*, Laxman has drawn three lines warning his sister-in-law, the epic heroine, Sita, not to cross them lest the evil should overcome her. This myth well suits the theme of the poem. Mahapatra also uses from the Australian Aboriginal myth of the first sunrise (Tukumbri's call) and from the aborigine myth of mother's milk settling into the milky way.

Althrough his poetic development, Mahapatra has skilfully employed myths, images and symbols in keeping with the changing modes of his poetry. His poetry is rich with thought provoking images (sometimes far fetched) and dynamic symbols that keep on changing as his muse advances. Bruce King makes an interesting observation when he says.

"While Mahapatra's world is filled with personal pain, guilt, remorse, hunger, desire and moments of renewal, his environment is filled with symbols of belief by the ordinary lives of the people of Cuttack, the temples, the Hindu festivals, the ancient monuments. The poems are varied attempts to bridge an epistemological, phenomenological gap to know, be part of enclose, experience, with the world and the other, whether it be a woman, temple stones, a Hindu priest. The skies, the wind, time and waves are symbols of the world of change and flux and which raise questions of nature and purpose of life as represented by the unchanging, fixed, rooted (stones, trees, the past) but these questions can never be answered by the mind, its perceptions and emotions."[17]

Sometimes we take recourse to recalling the old myths to explain away our failure and get solace at the time of defeat. Mahapatra takes digs at such an attitude in *Burden of Waves and Fruit*:

> "Would we go on gnawing at our old myths
> arguing with the vital organs of body and mind
> to approach only the rear entrance to the page
> surrounded by the expansive air of defeat?
> Or was it wise to emerge from sleep,
> doing what we could into the light that still had time
> stretched out before us?

Mahapatra himself acknowledges the vital role of imagery in his poetry. Though his poetry is neither thought-oriented like Ezekiel's nor it is image-oriented like Ramanujan's, it takes both the imagery and thought content together and integrates them to reveal meaning. Hence, one has to take both 'signification' (meaning of words according to linguistic code) and 'value' (meaning of words in their context,) as Widdowson would say into consideration to dive deep into the inner resources of his poetry. That is perhaps the reason why his poetry appears to be difficult, complex and obscure.

Coming to the form in his poetry it can be said with certainty that he avoids the rigors of metrical verse. He, like most of the Indian English poets writes in free verse. The stanza pattern is irregular and the style is elliptical. There is no regular rhyming scheme and the tone is almost colloquial and conversational. But the reading of his poems is not clogged by clumsiness. The words are often difficult like Shiv K. Kumar's and the imagery is difficult—so also the symbols.

But the voice that speaks through them is sincere and thoroughly honest. There is no attempt at camouflaging and irony is almost absent in his poetry. In his attempt to come to terms with himself, Mahapatra sees the world with detachment and comprehends the reality that he encounters in the modern world and portrays it objectively. He tries, to evoke the native tradition and myths of the land with its recurrent symbols in his poetry in order to recreate the past in modern terms. There is no attempt at sentimentalizing the past but he tries to evoke the Indian tradition and write poetry keeping India in his bones. At the same time, he is not oblivious of the present as past and present together form new wholes in his poetry.

## NOTES

1. Jayanta Mahapatra, *Face to Face with the Contemporary Poem*, ACLALS Bulletin/ Newsletter, IX, April 1981, p. 10.
2. Jayanta Mahapatra, *Tenor* NOI, June 1978, pp. 61-62.
3. Jayanta Mahapatra, *Face to Face with Contemporary Poem*, p. 9.
4. *Ibid.*, p. 11.
5. *Ibid.*, p. 10.
6. Quoted by M.K. Naik, "The Two Worlds of Imagery" *The Poetry of Jayanta Mahapatra: A Critical Study* (ed.) Madhusudan Prasad (New Delhi: Sterling Publishers 1986), p. 99.
7. *Ibid.*, pp.103-4.
8. Jayanta Mahapatra, "An Orissa Journal" *Queen's Quarterly,* Canada, Spring LXXX, I, 1973, p. 72.
9. K. Ayyappa Panikar, 'The Poetry of Jayanta Mahapatra' *OJES,* Vol. XI11, No. 1, 1977, pp. 132-33.
10. V.A. Shahane, "The 'Naked Earth' and Beyond: The Poetry of Jayanta Mahapatra" *Perspectives on Indian Poetry in English* (ed) M.K. Naik (New Delhi Abhinav Publications, 1984), p. 147.
11. S.K. Desai, 'The Poetic Craft', *The Poetry of Jayanta Mahapatra: A Critical Study,* p. 126.
12. Ajit Khullar, "Relationship': Analysis and Influences", *The Poetry of Jayanta Mahapatra: A Critical Study,* p. 195.
13. Jayanta Mahapatra, ' The Voice in the Ink', *The Illustrated Weekly of India,* April 1, 1990, p. 28.
14. Frank Allen, 'Crisis of Belief, *Parnassus* (Spring/Summer 1981), p. 335.
15. Jayanta Mahapatra, *Notes* to *Temple* (Sydney: Dangaroo Press, 1989), p. 56.
16. *Ibid.*
17. Bruce King, *Modern Indian poetry in English* (Delhi: O.U.P. 1987), p. 206.

# The Making of Indian English Idiom

4

POETRY written in English today in different countries of the world is not regarded as English Poetry, for the identity of a literature is based not on language but on nationality and culture. Poets all over the world who write their poetry in English do not write in the same way. The language is English but the expression and mode of collocations are different. That is why literatures written in English in Canada, Australia and America are known as Canadian literature, Australian literature and American literature respectively but not as English literature or part of English literature. Hence, the Indian English writer is judged by the intensity of his Indianness. This identification will be possible only when Indian English is treated as a distinct idiom. Our contemporary Indian English poets are aware of this problem and also making efforts in the direction of establishing Indian English as a distinct variety of English free of Anglo-American influence. Poets like Nissim Ezekiel, R. Parthasarathy, Kamala Das, P. Lal, Shiv K. Kumar, Keki N. Daruwalla, A.K. Ramanujan, Jayanta Mahapatra and a few others are creating a new Indian English idiom in their poetry that is at once recognizable from British, American, Canadian and Australian English. Jayanta Mahapatra's contribution to the creation of Indian English idiom is immense.

Mahapatra's use of language is interwoven with his growth as a poet through successive books of verse. Poetry for him is a craft that needs to be chiselled. In his poetry, both theme and technique go together as he experiments with language poem after poem in trying to acquire inwardness with it. He is capable of using English language with passionate precision that helps him to establish his identity as India's foremost poet in English.

Two questions need to be examined in the poetry of Mahapatra: One, how does he compose his poems? and two, how does he use 'English' in his poetry? I think, the answer to these two questions will reveal the making of Indian English idiom in Mahapatra's poetry. Let us examine the first question which obviously leads to another question: does Mahapatra have a theory of poetry of his own?

In an article titled 'The Voice in the Ink' (*The Illustrated Weekly of India,* April 1, 1990) Mahapatra gives a clue to his idea of poetry in the following words:

"One does not know what poetry is, or what poetry does—but that, like metaphysics, poetry persists in trying to find something of permanence beyond changing appearances, some yet unknown form of a transcendent nature."

His idea of writing poetry is to juxtapose the opposites in the context of a poem. Perhaps, like W.B. Yeats, Mahapatra believes that without contraries there is no progression. He wants to break a new ground in poetry by deviating from his predecessors. This is clearly stated in the following lines:

> Would we go on gnawing at our old myths,
> arguing with the vital organs of body and mind,
> to approach only the rear entrance to the page,
> surrounded by the expansive air of defeat?
> or was it wise to emerge from sleep,
> doing what we could, into the light .../...

Poetry being a mental activity inevitably takes the image of the human being into its orbit—consciously or otherwise. Mahapatra's poetry records his interaction with the outerworld and his environment. Mahapatra, for example, gives an account of young American men and women in a poem titled, "The Lost Children of America" and tells us how he wrote it: "The Lost Children of America" written some years ago, the lines came about from those sights which were common in the city of mine in those days. Before me, the high bank of the river, where the smoke of funeral pyres trembles the leaves of the pipals: before me too, a white couple walking hand in hand, apparently visitors from lands beyond our seas. I observe them: shabbily attired, their hairs unkempt, they move about barefoot as though they exist in dreams of their own. And it made me wonder why is it that these affluent men and women from the west chose to live the poverty-ridden air of India, to make me write this poem and wonder at the truth of life." (*The Illustrated Weekly of India,* April 1, 1990, P- 29)

> I have no need to ask
> why they come ten thousand miles,
> for though their eyes are open they appear asleep
> for they too are men with dreams.

An encounter with these American youngmen and women brings a kind of interaction between the poet and them. Perhaps, that provides an opportunity to know each other and may be an occasion to criticise each other. Thus, the poet writes:

> We gaze at each other in Silence, the lost child and I
> who knows who is playing a joke on whom?

Mahapatra often ponders over the question of the value of poetry in a poem called "Last Night the Poem'!

> But what use is a poem, once the writing's done?
> Words looking for what, in the dark of the soul?
> Like the sound of a match striking, then over,
> I know that much. When all else has failed
> the poem's words are perhaps justified.

What Mahapatra means is that a poem should evoke a kind of experience in the minds of the readers which went into the making of the poem. True, a poem cannot be successfully paraphrased nor does it have a single meaning. A poem, conveys a kind of experience, may be a situation which could be interpreted in more than one sense. In an ambiguous manner he asks a number of questions with reference to the nature of poetry in a poem called, "Will a poem of mine be the only Answer"?

> Will the poem of mine be the only answer?
> Will its words make me feel something
> I do not want to forget?

... ... ... ...
... ... ... ...
All this naked knowledge makes me tremble,
defeated as I am by my own tactics, my poetry
by the words I measure with my pain.

Here is a contrast. When Eliot measures out our lives with coffee spoons, Mahapatra tries to measure out his pain with words that make his poems. In other words, there is an attempt to integrate his personal experience with the contemporary situation to give it a general symbol. This reminds us of Eliot's comment on W.B. Yeats. There are a number of ways in which a poet can give a distinct touch and an identity to his poetry. He can do it by acclimatizing an indigenous tradition to a language other than one's first language (and in Mahapatra's case, English) and by way of evocating the place to which he belongs. This commitment to locale is seen in Whitman's nineteenth century New York, Robert Frost's New England, W.B. Yeats's Sligo and Nissim Ezekiel's Bombay. Similarly Mahapatra's locale is the golden triangle—Cuttack, Bhubaneswar and Puri which form the background of many of his poems. As a bilingual poet, Mahapatra faces the dilemma of choosing a language as the medium of his poetry and answers:

"... I am in love with English. And then, my Schooling was in English and I learnt my language from British School-masters —mainly from English novels; so blame H. Rider Haggard and Edgar Rice Burroughs and Ballantyne from whom I caught the first delight of words gravid with meaning. Further, I feel I can express myself better in English than in Oriya. And, I have done a lot of translations, in verse, from the Oriya."[1]

It is not that always a writer chooses a medium, but the medium too chooses a writer. Mahapatra's choice of English as the medium of poetry has given a new dimension to Indian English idiom. Like Ezekiel, P. Lal, Kamala Das, A.K. Ramanujan, Shiv K. Kumar, Mahapatra too contributes substantially to the creation of a new Indian English idiom. His use of English language has been influenced by his scientific knowledge. He often uses the language in an erratic and arbitrary manner. From the beginning of his poetic career,

Mahapatra lays emphasis on the language of poetry by employing new images and using rhetoric in his poetry. Take for instance an early poem like 'The Faith'. He has used an unusual collocation of words in describing the Puri temple.

> That sentence of old
> moves him towards the furious wrinkled walls?
> The Puri priest standing in indulgent sunshine
>
> Plays a small ridicule across the melting festival
> Safe in place above a pile of hard eyed ancestors.

The use of humanizing epithets for inanimate nouns like 'furious wrinkled walls' 'indulgent sunshine' and 'melting festival' is deliberate. He tries to create an impression on the minds of readers by using such unconventional epithets.

Mahapatra successfully conveys the desire for sex being fulfilled by taking advantage of hunger in a typical manner in a poem called 'Hunger'. Ayyappa Paniker rightly suggests that the economy of words heightens the meaning of the poem. He is full of appreciation of the way Mahapatra chooses his idiom. Thus, he writes:

"A profoundly human document this poem is, and its power depends mainly on the authenticity of the experience established by the words and their arrangement. Every word is telling, is in its proper place. One could hardly wish to upset any sequence in it. The happy blending of the literal and the metaphorical is achieved in experience like 'the flesh was heavy on my back', 'trailing his nets and his nerves', 'the white bone thrash his eyes', 'burning the house I lived in', 'the flickering dark', 'his lean too opened like a wound', 'a father's exhausted will', 'her years were cold as rubber' etc. The protagonist, the fisherman and the girl have the clarity and hardness of figures in bas-relief. The complexity of the human situation is not sacrificed for the sake of any sociological formula. The poet achieves his eloquence through silence."[2]

In one of his early but well-known poems titled "The Whorehouse in a Calcutta Street" Mahapatra tries to recreate a character in a typical Indian situation.

Walk right in. It is yours,
Where the house smiles wryly into the lighted street
Think of the women
wished to know and haven't!
.... .... .... ....
Are you ashamed to believe you're in this?

.... .... .... ....
Even the women don't wear them —
like jewels or precious stones at the throat,
the faint feeling deep at a Woman's Centre
that brings back the discarded things:
the little turnings of blood
at the far edge of the rainbow
You fall back against her in the dumb light
trying to learn something more about women —
while she does that she thinks proper to please you,
the sweet, the little things, the imagined;
.... .... .... ....
.... .... .... ....
...., her words close behind
'Hurry, will you? let me go'
and her lonely breath thrashed against your kind.

The poem begins with the instruction to the protagonist how to find a whorehouse in a Calcutta Street and ends with the woman asking him to leave when she is in a hurry to receive new customers. The expressions like 'the little turnings of blood/at the far edge of the rainbow', and 'her lonely breath thrashed against your kind' are highly suggestive and evocative of the sexual act one is supposed to perform in a whorehouse. Mahapatra uses language in a typical Indian way to bring alive the portrait of the woman who is supposed to be involved in the physical union with the protagonist.

Using English language in subtle way to bend and modulate the rhythms of it to the needs and nuances of Indian experience, Mahapatra tries to come to terms with Hindu mythology and its celebration of the belief that the universe is boundlessly various, that everything occurs simultaneously, that all possibilities may exist without excluding each other. Religious ceremony as it is understood today in the West, is fundamentally different from Indian concept which takes it as an internal symbol of timelessness. In the words of Frank Allen, 'Religious ceremony to the contemporary West, largely synonymous with dubiety and self-denial, evokes a peace that passeth understanding. To use it, the poet must struggle to free this symbolism from cultural prejudice and fantasy. Not so for India. The Hindu ethos has given all diverse human impulses, no matter how anarchic, undignified or bizarre, a valid and accessible place in its beliefs."[3]

Apart from concentrating on beliefs and rituals, Mahapatra also makes use of the current situation in contemporary society to give his poetry a distinct Indian flavour and create a new Indian English idiom. It is in this aspect that Mahapatra is in the company of Nissim Ezekiel, Shiv K. Kumar, R. Parthasarathy, Kamala Das and O.P. Bhatnagar who underline this typical Indian sensibility in their poetry. K. Ayyappa Paniker has rightly stressed this point in the following words:

"Indian poetry in English necessarily refers to two parameters: Indian and English. 'Indian' may mean, either written by Indian citizens or written about Indian subjects or even expressing Indian sensibility. This implies that there is a sensibility that is identified with the land and the people of India. National sensibilities are ultimately based on racial and cultural factors. Whether they are inherited or acquired is another moot question."[4]

Jayanta Mahapatra's *Relationship* (1981) and two recent volumes *Burden of Waves and Fruit* (1988) and *Temple* (1989) reveal a distinct Indian sensibility that immediately arrests one's attention. History, myths, legends, folklore all go together to establish a distinct idiom and identity in these volumes. The publisher's note to *Burden of Waves and Fruit* rightly stresses this aspect:

"There are many rivers in these works, much rain and Sun, long evenings and a few dawns—occasionally, there are intimate glimpses of friends, lovers and a son. India is everywhere and nowhere."[5]

To my mind *Relationship* is a very successful poem that reveals an Indian sensibility and in a way creates an Indian English idiom. The poem is set in Orissa and the history and myth of Mahapatra's land of birth are built into the texture of this poem. It at once gives a kind of identity to Indian English poetry by acclimatizing an indigenous tradition to English language.

The first section of the poem though overworked with images succeeds in conveying the impossibility of unravelling the mystery of life. The heroic past of the land of Orissa has been revoked with a sense of pride.

> Time
> and the boat,
> and the initiation into the mystery of peace,
> the sailing ships of those maritime ancestors,
> who have vanished in the black Bay without a trace,
> that only live in the sound of the waves
> flinging themselves into the dark fringes
> of this land from Chilika to Chandipur.

(*Relationship* 1)

The first section of the poem serves as an exposition when references are made to the Mahanadi, the prime river of the State, the temple of Konarka, the ancient harbours like Chilika and Chandipur. There is search for roots and the heroic Oriya past is vividly remembered and recalled with a sense of nostalgia. The glory and pride of our ancestors exhibited in the climactic Kalinga War in 261 B. C. which turned Ashok, the Great into a deeply religious man is now a long lost trait in our racial character and behaviour. The river Daya is a witness to our ancestor's heroic effort which has become a sort of myth for us. Once heroic and militant race is now no more than a mere memory, for its successors proved to be unworthy of keeping the glory of their ancestors afloot and drifted away from their ideals. Thus, the poem begins with a sense of dispossession and gradually moves towards rootedness—leading from guilty deprivation and hurtful otherness to a joyful sense of being re-united with one's origin and source.

*Relationship* explores into the past indicating that one of the most rewarding strategies for Indian English poet is 'Only connect'[6]. Konarka plays a very significant role in the poetry of Jayanta Mahapatra linking the past with the present and initiating a dialogue with the future. Unlike R.K. Narayan's Malgudi, Konarka is a real temple that stands as a backdrop to *Relationship*. Thus, Mahapatra writes:

as I forget easily
my old village's pelt, glistening with rain
and the stillness of my gentle daughter's skin
forget the desire
oozing out of the lewn stones of Konarka.

(*Relationship*)

From the ruins of Konarka temple, Mahapatra takes us down the memory lane to our 'maritime ancestors' who brought glory for the State. Time has withered away everything but the racial memory haunts the poet without end. Since 'time has no mouth', the poet being caught up 'in the currents of time' watches the 'blue sky/seep out slowly', not knowing 'whether the earth/would let me find finally its mouth'. The Mahanadi, Konarka, and 'maritime ancestors' remind the poet of a glorious past of the land of his birth and the poet writes with a sense of belonging:

Only that the stones were my own,
waiting as mother or goddess or witch
as my birth feeds on them
as though on the empty dugs of sorcerous thought.

(*Relationship*)

Apart from the Mahanadi and Konarka temple, river Daya too is a silent witness to our ancestor's heroic act all through the ages. In a bid to get an identity that is lovable and enduring, the poet contrasts the present depicting the sense of helplessness with a sense of certainty and pride that our ancestors had in the past. To think, it hurts and the poet is at a loss to comprehend the fall in the life of a race that was grand and heroic once upon a time. Living in an irreligious milieu the sense of 'empty sadness' turning into 'the mangled skeleton of a sleep' disappoints the poet and the purpose of life seems to be meaningless and a burden which makes him realise the futility of such an existence. Thus, the poet broods over the problem and there is an element of introspection when he says,

> It is my own life
> that has cornered me beneath the stones
> of this temple in ruins, in a blaze of sun.
>
> (*Relationship*)

Mahapatra's poetry counters whatever distorts the image of man and integrates the highest form of thought with deepest intuition of freedom. He judges political issues from humanistic point of view. His *Dispossessed Nests* is a bright illustration of this point of view. There are only two long poems in this volume: 'Bewildered Wheatfields' (23 Sections) and "A Dance of Bejewelled Snakes" (12 Sections) which depict the predicament of human life in our time in India. Irony is the key note of contemporary situation in which the poet watches the T.V. and shudders:

> Another death?
> little pile of ash
> uncurls
> like a woken beast.
>
> (*Dispossessed Nests,* p. 17)

A sense of grief and uncertainty overtakes the poet when he sees senseless deaths and violence on T.V. Thus, he says.

> Here
> I do not know
> what I am looking for.
>
> Rain falls heavy, hard as stones,
> I am so far away from these falls.
> I chance pain and prayer,
> the simple pendulum,
> trying my utmost to replace
> the senseless refrain of hate
> by the amazement to be alive.
>
> (*Dispossessed Nests,* p. 20)

Life in Punjab has become risky and the value of it has been lost upon the people who perpetuate violence and innocent killings.

The image of India as a heroic land is crumbling with the onslaught of terrorism. The poet becomes nostalgic for a moment and a sense of despair overwhelms him.

> This country urges us to seek the stars at night
> too full as we are of mythic battles, angry gods
> and the heroism of Hanuman. Upon those
> distant pin-points of light we might reconstruct
> some other world, denying memory, journeying
> no more. None. Ah love, we had read so much
> about you, about freedom. Was everything you did,
> Gandhiji, only an act you put on for posterity?
> With India, our India, barely worth roping?
>
> (*Dispossessed Nests,* p. 44)

Politics being a metaphor for life in the present day world, the poet reflects on the contemporary situation giving it as it were, 'a local habitation and a name'. In a typical Indian way, the poet records his disappointment in the following lines:

> So many things,
> as the country's leaders wait for a sign,
> and a future this present will not enable us
> to live in.
> ... ... ... ... ...
> ... ... ... ... ...
> When we learn to let
> Our minds leave us, we do not care where
> true feeling lies, or for a country's
> national anthem floating around in counterfeit freedom
> its time moves to echo the rain-voice
> lying too deep for our nerves' reach, besieging
> in vain the poet's lonely walls.
>
> (*Dispossessed Nests,* p. 45)

Only an Indian English poet could express his feelings in such a situation in this typical coinage like 'Counterfeit freedom' 'rain-voice', and 'nerves reach'. Typical imagery, simile and collocation of words in Mahapatra's poetry go a long way to create distinct

Indian English idiom. The decline in Indian life shatters the dream of the poet. As the poet puts it:

> The leaves of the dark tree of India
> are gasping for breath
> across the green air.
>
> An awe circles and chases a tale
> through the leaves, a star
> looks fixed in space's old embrace.
>
> And I have a dream.
> It is like a school boy in a class room
> who has not understood what teacher is saying
> but puts on a knowing smile for all to believe
>
> (*Dispossessed Nests,* p. 48)

Collocations like 'green air', an owl 'chases a tale', and comparisons such as 'a dream' like the pretentious smile of a school boy who has not understood his teacher in the classroom are typical of Indian English poet. These uses distinguish Indian English poetry from other poetry written in English all over the world. India is a country which has no dearth of leaders and gods. He ridicules a typical habit of Indian people to turn to government and pray to God for anything and everything they hope to acquire or desire to get. Mahapatra puts this aspect of Indian people in a subtle artistic manner with an implicit irony. Thus, he writes:

> For if anything happens,
> their dreams of belief tell them that—their gods
> and their government shall take care of them.
>
> (*Dispossessed Nests,* p. 54)

Mahapatra has a laborious style of writing. As a rule, he revises and perhaps re-revises his poems. Vocabulary is taken from Science and from other branches of learning to make his poetry deliberately difficult for the common readers. In India, poetry readers particularly, Indian English poetry readers are few and far between. An Indian English poet is never seriously read unless his poetry is prescribed for a class. He may get the attention of the readers, if he wins a prize of national or

international importance. Mahapatra knows it too well. He is a conscious artist who looks 'before and after' and perhaps does not pine for readers. His poetry appears to be difficult because of its difficult vocabulary, far-fetched images and contrived style. For instance, he likens the 'feel' of a 'heart' to 'a hot ball of lead'. Expressions like 'brimful of light', 'heart's sack', 'battered body', 'charred skills', 'unattainable smile', 'bewildered wheat fields', 'impatient darkness', 'shakuni-skies', 'indulgent lie', 'tumours of noiseless tears', 'the incinerated sun', 'knowledges', 'labyrinth', 'an evening of claustral shadow', 'wanton nightmare' 'bastard past', 'golden smoke', 'ambiguous abandon', 'frantic waters', 'the blood-oracle's fatality', 'unmilked cows', 'wispynets', 'untroubled distance', 'bejewelled snakes', 'endless wound', 'music of blood', 'hypnotised feelings' which are found in *Dispossessed Nests* are new to Indian English poetic diction. These expressions may sound un-English (the feature is certainly un-English) but they indicate that the Indian English idiom is in the making.

His other important books *Relationship, Life Signs, Burdens of Waves and Fruit* and *Temple* contain numerous expressions which are un-English in feature but new to Indian English vocabulary. A good number of Jayanta Mahapatra's poems have their roots in day-to-day common experience. He has made an excellent use of English language in his poetry. His 'A Letter to Kazuka Shirajshi in Tokyo' is rooted in day-to-day common experience and has conversational language. The first few lines have a conversational tone.

> It's rain again. Going on and on all day,
> like hunger. You would think this country
> has nothing, but seven hundred million bellies.

M. Tarinayya gives an interesting account of the opening lines of this poem in the following words:

"But 'It's rain again...like hunger's—the unexpected comparison between 'rain' and 'hunger' gives us a jolt. Here is what the Prague School of Linguists call 'organised violation' of 'standard language'—a deautomatization which demands a corresponding deautomatization of response. Rain, the ancient symbol of fertility appears to the poet as anything but life-giving. Monsoon rain and hunger, both elemental—one of impersonal nature and the other man-made and of the human body—are both paradoxically ever present realities in India. It is the second of those two realities, hunger, as though it were impersonal like the incessant rain which the foreigner sees and hears about and hence, the poet says that Kazuka Shiraishi who is in Tokyo, one of the world's technologically and scientifically advanced metropolitan cities 'would think that this country has nothing but six hundred million bellies'.[7]

In this poem, Mahapatra digs at our so-called socialism casual attitude to love and sex and finally blind belief and superstition. The language he uses here is very apt and it conveys the underneath irony without any violence.

> I am one of them, listening to the radio each day
> and learning more about fertilizers and democracy
> and of the tightening of jaw muscles that builds out
> of a hastily-induced abortion. (Not that abortions
> haven't been legalised here, you know.)

The greatness of Mahapatra's poetry lies in the power it imparts to us to see men and women, our own contemporaries in their true colours. One such situation given in the poem, "30th January, 1982: A Story" lays bare the hypocrisy of our people who pay lip service to Mahatma Gandhi's cult of non-violence but do not practise it. Thus, Mahapatra writes:

> Another day like any other.
> The bleating goat on the butcher's block
> quickened its last breath and stared wide-eyed.
> Its cry bent deeper still over the fringe of its death
> while the butcher worried that his knife
> was fast losing its sharpness..
> At this moment the mobile loudspeaker van
> of the Department of Public Relations swept past
> Pouring out the words of Gandhi's once-favourite
> hymn.

(*Burden of Waves and Fruit*, p. 26)

The undertone of irony is typical of this situation which unmasks the gap between preaching and practising in modern Indian life. The tone is conversational and there is an ever-present liquidness of movement in his language recapturable in Indian life.

Mahapatra has an eye for the right word in the right place. The style may appear to be laborious but the choice of words heighten the meaning of his poem. Here are a few examples from different poems:

> the acid sounds of a distant bell
>
> ('Dawn', *A Rain of Rites,* p. 1)

> The familiar words are rude like roots and out of place
> hanging like history in which one's sky stumbles.
>
> ('Ceremony', *A Rain of Rites,* p. 15)

> In a corner of her mind
> a living green mango
> drops softly to earth.
>
> ('Summer', *A Rain of Rites,* p. 14)

> You fall back against her in the dumb light,
> trying to learn something more about women—
> while she does what she thinks proper to please you,
> the sweet, the little things, the imagined;
> until the statue of the man within
> you've believed in throughout the years
> comes back to you, a disobeying toy —
>
> (*The Whorehouse in a Calcutta Street*)

> All day and all night I am moved by myself,
> only the tree that is there,
> the axes of seasons in a derelict eye
>
> ('A Tree', *A Rain of Rites*)

> His mind, like the sun,
> gently climbs the godly hill of day,
> will not touch or reveal,
> the many levels
> of himself.
>
> (*Somewhere, My Man*)

The face
which knows it's doomed, balanced as a precarious sun-set?
or had I found at least the success in my quiet life, hanging
like a puppet on a string in a pantomime, indifferent to
another life in the faces of others?

(*The Face*)

The lines quoted above show an unusual collocation of words such as 'acid sounds of distant bell', 'words are rude like roots', 'dumblight', 'a disobeying toy' (referring to male genital), 'axes of seasons', 'derelict eye', 'godly hill of day', 'precarious sun set' and typical Indian expression like 'living green mango' dropping on the earth from the corner of one's mind. His vocabulary is both scientific and laboured.

The shadow of T.S. Eliot looms large in the use of Mahapatra's language in poetry. However, he gives an Indian twist to it. Here are a few examples:

And a man begins to begin again
in the centre of this past,
and sees no end of it.

(*Samsara*)

Somewhere
a door opens and shuts,
years elapse quietly behind,
like things
people have known all along.

(*Somewhere, My Man*)

Where you sit, in snide dreaming,
you have your own death.
What is this thing which won't let you sit back
which you cannot share?

(*The Landscape of Return*)

What one endures
and one will continue to endure, a kind of world
that comes up of all the love he has known,
so that man can see from the vast night around him
the beauty soar into the sky,

> into the tangles of cloud and rain,
> of that drowsy, voice calling
> from other people's lives
>
> (*Relationship*)

Mahapatra's use of language in the 'rain poems' are reminiscient of Eliot. The following lines are cases in point:

> What holds my rain so it's hard to overcome?
>
> (*A Rain of Rites*)

> The clear, wise eyes of water, running,
> The look on the other side of life
>
> (*A Rain*)

> In the rain that sails vast spaces
> towards the season's end, ............
> .... .... .... .... ....
> .... .... .... .... ....
> Thus I approach the boundary between
> the voices I make and their dropping echoes,
> facing those secrets lost in one's own creation,
> now to fold slowly, or rise and fall in turn,
> in that inner kingdom of consciousness
> which moves each torture of memory into the flesh
>
> (*Four Rain Poems*)

> do I know what really is my loss,
> do I know that I mean when I say this
> while the remembered rain beats against my walls?
>
> (*Four Rain Poems*)

Mahapatra's rain poems 'enact in Eliot's style, the death of water, death of air and death of light'.[8]

Mahapatra has in a way succeeded in acclimatizing English language to an indigenous tradition. His use of Indian imagery and symbols in English language in his own way, has contributed to the growth of an Indian English Idiom. A creative writer has the right to use and twist a language in his own way and to his own advantage. Jayanta Mahapatra like other important Indian English poets Nissim Ezekiel, P. Lal, R. Parthasarathy and Kamala Das, has twisted English language to suit his themes.

Unusual collocation of words gives a distinct colour to Mahapatra's poetry. Here are a few examples:

> A rape penetrates the periphery of the jungle.
> And thought looks up
> dumbly at the toes of words.
>
> (*Events*)

> Sometimes at night
> When all voices die
> my mind sees earth, my country
> .... .... .... .... ....
> .... .... .... .... ....
> Wherever I try to live
> in pious pretence at Puri
> or in the fiery violence of a revolutionary
> my reason becomes a prejudiced sorrow
> like socialism
>
> (*A Country*)

> And now we will endure the pain
> when the words of our songs droop like lilies
> in the dark without standing in judgment —
> passing by the abandoned cocoon
> through the stench of blood over the pure down wall
> across stinging smoke burnt-out doubts:
> perhaps like ageing men
> in their bitter-lemon gaze who look up wearily
> from their doorsteps when the truth-light
> of day is levelling.
>
> (*The Lost Children of America*)

The deliberate effort to collocate words like, 'rape penetrates', 'thought looks up', 'toes of words', 'pious pretence', 'fiery violence' 'prejudiced sorrow', 'songs drop like lilies', 'burnt-out doubts', 'bitter-lemon gaze' and 'truth-light' makes his style laborious and phoney. There is a desire on his part to emphasize his subject by making new coinages. This is typical of Indian English poets to make unusual collocation of words in their poetry to give it a distinct identity. They also tend to exaggerate. But rhetoric like hyperbole is not their cup of tea. They use adjectives that normally do not go with the nouns they are supposed to qualify. Hence, they produce a peculiar sound which are jarring to the ears. In Mahapatra's case, the style becomes verbose.

Mahapatra's poetry is not image-oriented like Ramanujan's and Shiv K. Kumar's poetry but it is thought-provoking like the poetry of O.P. Bhatnagar and Nissim Ezekiel—particularly the latter's *Unfinished Man, The Exact Name* and *Hymns in Darkness.* But Mahapatra's use of language is different from that of Nissim Ezekiel. He uses some of the scientific words and his imagery is often drawn from Science. He is to some extent successful in conveying his thought content through his deliberate choice of difficult words in a verbose style. However, it may be said to his credit that like R. Parthasarathy, Arun Kolatkar and A. K. Ramanujan, Jayanta Mahapatra has acclimatized the native Oriya tradition to English language. Hence, in his poetry one sees the growth of an Indian English idiom, which makes his poetry distinct from poetry written in English in other countries of the world.

## NOTES

1. Jayanta Mahapatra, 'Inner View', *Tenor* (Hyderabad, June 1978, p. 59).
2. K. Ayyappa Paniker, 'The Poetry of Jayanta Mahapatra', *Osmania, Journal of English Studies* (1977) 13 : 1, p. 122.
3. Frank Allen, *Parnassus* (Spring/Summer, 1981): p. 335.
4. K. Ayyappa Paniker, "Indian Poetry in English and the Indian Aesthetic Tradition", *The Indian Journal of English Studies,* 23 (1983), p. 137.
5. Publisher's Note to *Burden of Waves and Fruits* (Washington D.C., 1988).
6. M.K. Naik, 'Only Connect', *Indian Book Chronicle,* January 1982, p. 16.
7. M. Tarinayya, "Jayanta Mahapatra's 'A Letter to Kazuka Shiraishi in Tokyo': An Analysis", *The Literary Criterion:* 20 : 3 (1985), pp. 61-62.
8. F.A. Inamdar, "The Symbolic Mode in Poetry", *The Poetry of Jayanta Mahapatra: A Critical Study,* New Delhi: Sterling Publishers, 1986, p. 262.

# A Critique of *A Whiteness of Bone*

5

JAYANTA MAHAPATRA'S thirteenth book of poems, *A Whiteness of Bone* was published by Viking [Penguin Books India (P) Ltd.] in 1992. It contains 59 poems on a wide range of subjects. Landscape, time and contemporary reality seem to have attracted him most and he creates a good many poems on and about them. Time theme which Mahapatra dealt with in *The False Start* and to some extent in *Relationship* resurfaces once again. Unlike Eliot's conception of time in which past, present and future meet at a point which is always 'present', Mahapatra's conception of time does not always have a simultaneous existence. It is spatial.

The first poem in this collection, 'Silent in the Valleys' sets the tone of the book by laying emphasis on time. Yesterday's child is today's man. But the toys, he played with during his childhood remain where they were. They remind him of his past and he can not meet them truly except in a flashback. In other words, the toys are symbols of one's past and they live in his memory. Time has created a wall between the toys and the adult human beings. This poem is an oblique poem which states one thing in terms of another. We know the innocence of one's childhood is lost as one grows into a man and acquires new experiences. In other words, we, human beings, change but the toys like a child remain for ever innocent. Time changes us but not the toys. Mahapatra writes:

> Toys are unaware how we grow
> They live near our childhoods

... ...
All I saw at first was time, gentle crystal
passing through the generations,
to touch or hug or break, against subterfuge
How they remain, silent in the valleys.

(*Silent in the Valleys*)

The toys can be taken as a symbol of a living past that haunts the poet without end. The poet realizes that memory of the inescapable past could be disturbing. He writes:

The past
lies everywhere, like water
I listen for moments to fill my life:

(*Afternoon*)

We move in time because we are born in time and we shall die in time. But sometimes people die prematurely. Mahapatra likens 'Time' to a green mango—for it has two alternatives. First, it may grow and ripe and second, it may drop from the tree without being ripe. Similarly, some people ripe with age and die living their life to the full and others pass away without being ripe. Being apprehensive of an untimely death the poet says, 'my death urges at the wrong time'. The image of time as a 'green mango' is an original one and it is adequate to the idea the poet seeks to convey.

In an Eliotian sense, Mahapatra takes time as a great healer. The wound caused by failure in love life, or betrayal in life, or inability to know one's own heart or misunderstanding with others can be healed by time. Mahapatra writes:

and such a time that truth would be alone when mist
disappears into the clear winter sky worn out by
the bare soles of time itself.

(*December*)

'Time' for Mahapatra is very important in the sense that it makes us understand things better. It teaches us how to realize the importance of life. As Mahapatra puts it:

bone of time
that makes each one understand

how night is night, and through it
to enter the kingdom where Orion turns,
calm and certain, into neither darkness nor light.

Time is a great educator for it helps us to 'see into the life of things'.

Those who do not forget time, find it hard and unbearable. As Mahapatra puts it:

This time is not an easy one,
for us who cannot forget ourselves.

(*The Waiting*)

Mahapatra in his latest book of poems, *A Whiteness of Bone* moves from modernism to post-modernism by laying emphasis on the semantic indeterminancy. Like the post-structuralists, particularly the deconstructionist, Mahapatra believes that a text does not have a fixity of meaning and on the other hand, it has potentials for meaning and it admits of several interpretations. Again like a post-modernist poet, Mahapatra seems to agree with Derrida's theory that no work of literature whatsoever has been able to express exactly what it wanted to say, because of semantic indeterminancy of words. Mahapatra writes:

All right words of mine drift
nearing meaning but never finding it.

(*The Time Afterward*)

'Time' may unveil the meaning in its entirety someday, hopes Mahapatra and continues to write poems uninterrupted. Mahapatra knows that time is all pervasive for all human actions take place in time. Time often proves us wrong. Mahapatra rightly says,

Time catches us in the act
of straightening ourselves, as if to say
that what has happened.

(*The Naked Light*)

Time constantly reminds us of our past through our memory. The 'mystic carings of a religious past' haunts the poet without end. Mahapatra rightly puts it:

I stare at my door
overpowered by time.

(*Doors*)

Apart from the time theme which dominates, this volume, *A Whiteness of Bone,* other themes like 'Landscape' ironical observations on contemporary situation, journey of the 'self' and 'history' too are worked out here. Mahapatra like Nissim Ezekiel writes a good deal of situational poems. India's recent past is still fresh in our memory. Mahapatra writes about it in "Of Independence Day". "The Fifteenth of August", "A Sullen Balance" and "Red Roses for Gandhi".

The present condition of the country depresses the poet. He fondly remembers Indira Gandhi who fell to an assassin's bullet like Mahatma Gandhi. She rendered invaluable service to this country.

Mahapatra writes:

For a second I see Indira Gandhi...
I realize she's dead too
and that my young friend
sprawled across the day
is so full of heroism

Perhaps all of India
is not awake at this hour.

submerged in her immensely,
I know I too cannot get away.

Like a patient crocodile
she leaves her pray to rot into softness,
fastened beneath the roots
of some banyan of our heritage
that overhangs the river of our time.

(*A Sullen Balance*)

The problems that bedevils us are being lost sight of. Indira Gandhi's sacrifice is too big to be understood at the moment. Again, echoing Eliot ('The river is within us, the sea is all about us', *Four Quartets*), Mahapatra tells us about 'the river of our time' which will ultimately make us realise the magnitude of the problems we face today to keep our country united and help us to understand Indira Gandhi's sacrifice.

Mahapatra creates poetry out of contemporary situation. He encounters everyday reality with the insight of a scientist and portrays it with objectivity of a true artist. In "Red Roses for Gandhi", Mahapatra tells us how we have forgotten, Gandhi's ideals and relegated him to the background by observing his birthday to a mere ritual. The poem is occasioned by the immolation of eight students on October 2, 1990, the day of Gandhiji's birth anniversary. Time has changed. We mechanically perform rituals on his birthday without practising his ideals. Mahapatra observes:

> Those roses tremble in the Prime Minister's hands now
> as he steps carefully toward
> the bitten marble of silent years.

The significance of the past and the sacrifice of our ancestors are lost upon us. This state of affairs makes the poet gloomy and leads to self-questioning:

> And I ask myself,
> will life ever be the same again,
> would this day ever make us brood
> on a monument of sleep?

Turning to Gandhi, with a note of pathos and melancholy Mahapatra says,

> Ah day, how your lean and naked face
> leans on the country where
> sons and daughters burn in tongues of fire

Though Gandhi is shown here as a spent force who no longer inspires confidence among the people, in another poem he inspires Indians most. The poet writes:

> The photograph of Gandhi in the new airport lounge
> is more than forty years old
> Everytime I look into the old man's eyes,
> he calmly hands my promise back to me.
>
> (*The Fifteenth of August*)

Mahapatra reveals himself as a patriotic poet in *A Whiteness of Bone* by writing a number of poems on the problems faced by the country. He is conscious of keeping the image of the country alive. In the international field, our country should maintain impartiality and objectivity. He gives vent to his feelings in *Another Love Poem*. The opening line of the poem, sets the tone of it. It goes like this:

> This country lives, on its image

The world which is divided into several blocks is always troubled by the enmity of the countries against one another. Mahapatra writes:

> We have become stiff and cautious with each other
> as this country is with the U.S. and the USSR.

The poet suggests a remedy that is to be objective in your approach. Thus, Mahapatra asks:

> What if we had touched, the only way
> we could touch?
> What if we stand here in the middle of nowhere?
> In a country drugged with its image.
>
> (*Another Love Poem*)

Mahapatra's sense of patriotism and awareness of contemporary situation together give rise to his concern for the country. Time has brought a remarkable change in society. No longer the children are afraid of their parents. The generation gap has widened the credibility gap between parents and children. 'The wheel has turned a full circle", and the parents are now very much conscious of their position. As Mahapatra writes:

> We are careful to say nothing now
> to our children that might displease
> or provoke them.
>
> (*Of Independence Day*)

Mahapatra's poetry shows his concern for the society. That is why a rape here or a murder there upsets him. Man's cruelty to man has become the order of the day. Mahapatra laments such a situation in a poem called 'Dawn'.

Things are only going their way.
The dawn appears headless again.
The child has already come to know,
from who knows whom
that peace has gone, never to return.

(*Dawn*)

Mahapatra is becoming a pessimist. In another poem he says,

In all this land
dream is not like unending railway tracks.

Being conscious of reality that engulfs us day in and day out, Mahapatra realizes that, 'all lives are not equal'. Jayanta Mahapatra in his early poems makes an attempt to get into the roots by turning inward. It is in this sense, he is with A.K. Ramanujan, R. Parthasarathy and Kamala Das in trying to evoke a native tradition in English language. Most of his poems are set in Orissa. This makes Paniker to say: 'Jayanta Mahapatra is an Orissan poet writing in English' (Paniker, 1991 : 15). Mahapatra speaks to us of an indigenous tradition in his poetry particularly in *Relationship* (1980) and tries to extend it by his individual talent. Again Paniker harks on this point when he observes: 'Mahapatra resorts to local colour and cultural echoes while Daruwalla uses the open air both as cultural theme and backdrop' *(Ibidem:* 18). But Mahapatra has overcome his local obsession and native cultural preoccupation by using national myths in *Temple* and writing patriotic poems concerning the nation and on the Father of the nation in his latest book of verse, *A Whiteness of Bone*. Mahapatra seems to have transcended the place (Cuttack, Puri, Bhubaneswar the golden triangle) by writing about the country as a whole. Mahapatra writes about Bhopal (in *Dispossessed Nests*) Independence Day, Gandhiji and quite a few subjects concerning the whole of India. Like Ezekiel, he tries to identify himself with modern India so that he can speak with confidence and reach many a readers all through the country. Mahapatra broadens his thematic range here. Some of the poems strike us most by evoking contemporary situation. Mahapatra writes as usual in free verse. He uses simile frequently in most of the poems of this volume. Most of the characters in this volume are 'half guessed and half understood' like the characters of T.S. Eliot. Sometimes, the poet becomes evasive, ambiguous and difficult by choice. Mahapatra seems to be identifying himself both with modern India and the landscape of the country. He is not an ironist or a parodist like Ezekiel. He is truly a modern poet who creates his poems out of contemporary reality. He speaks to us in our situation and elicits our participation. His patriotic poems make an absorbing reading. On the whole *A Whiteness of Bone* appeals to us for its variety of themes and subtlety of expression, despite its occasional slips into ambiguity and obscurity.

## WORK CITED

Paniker, K. Ayyappa. *Modern Indian Poetry in English.* New Delhi: Sahitya Akademi, 1991.

# Poetry in the Mid-Nineties

6

JAYANTA MAHAPATRA has published two volumes of poems—*The Poetry of Jayanta Mahapatra* (1995) edited by P.P. Raveendran and *Shadow Space* (1997) in the mid-nineties. Close on the heels of the twenty-first century and a new millennium, he has also published a few significant poems in *Poetry Review* (London), *The Newyorker* (New York) and *Himal* (Kathmandu). The question is how to read these poems, particularly when post-colonial theory and cultural studies have become a fashion in the English speaking world. I think, we can read Mahapatra's latest poetry with pleasure and profit as post-colonial poetry, by applying post-colonial theory and cultural studies approach to it.

Jayanta Mahapatra as a post-colonial poet, writes to establish a native tradition by resisting the former coloniser and asserting national identity. The importance attached to the critique of Frantz Fanon, Edward Said, Gayatri Spivak and Homi K. Bhabha has resulted in the dissemination of post-colonial theory. If Edward Said and Gayatri Spivak emphasize culture and imperialism as the distinguished factors that influence post-colonial literature, Fredrick Jameson speaks of allegorical nature of this literature and underlines the history of the erstwhile British colonies (now free independent countries). Moreover, Jameson speaks in terms of binary opposition of the First and Third Worlds that results in the creation of post-colonial literature. Two important texts, *The Empire Writes Back* (1989) by Bill Ashcroft, Gareth Griffiths, and Helen Tiffin and *The Encyclopaedia of Post-colonial Literatures in English* (1994) edited by Benson and Connolly have popularised the term 'post-colonial' and lent respectability to post-colonial literature. Semantically post-colonialism means something that has a concern only with the national culture after the departure of imperial power. But in actual practice, it has to be understood only in reference to colonialism. Like colonialism, post-colonialism is a state of consciousness; a crucial stage in the continuum of our cultural process and self-awareness. Colonialism involves two types of imperialism—political and cultural. Therefore, myth and history, language and landscape, self and the other are all very important ingredients of post-colonialism.

I would like to begin my study of Mahapatra's recent poetry with one of his latest poems, titled, "A Pastoral Perhaps" (Published in *Poetry Review,* Vol. 89, No. 3 Autumn 1999, London), which reveals his concern for national identity and nationhood. The opening stanza of the poem depicts a village scene (India lives in her villages, said Gandhiji and rightly so) which is evocative of the spirit of true India.

> By the scummy pond, in the thin rain,
> a woman shakes her hair loose,
> before entering the water. Through the grove
> of bamboos dripping bright raindrops,
> a long abandoned thought appears to push a smile
> at her lips. Audacious shadows open
> to take her in; she shrugs, strong, unaware.

The image of a village woman entering into a pond, shaking her hair loose to have her bathe and the raindrops dripping through the bamboo grove, brings the rural India alive in the minds of the readers. The second stanza further reinforces the idea of true India lying in her villages, when the landscape of the place is integrated with history of the country—the past is dovetailed into the present and merges with it. Mahapatra writes:

> Leaves green, sway under the cloudy sky
> and only the woman's sunbronzed face looks out
> above the water. The air drops quietly back into the past,
> a part of the present seems to break away.

The destiny of India heaves in darkness,
in the memory of ancient waters.

The history of India is now in the pond where the women bathes it is in a way, re-locating the past in the present, a preoccupation of post-colonial writers (poets included). This is what Eliot did in a grandway in 'Little Gidding' *(Four Quartets)* Eliot writes:

A people without history
Is not redeemed from time, for history is a pattern
of timeless moments. So, while light fails
On a winter's afternoon, in a secluded chapel
History is now and England.

Jayanta Mahapatra tries to bring alive the past of his own country in a new Indian English idiom. It is in the line of the thesis that the writers of the epoch making book, *The Empire Writes Back* put forth—a re-assertion of nationhood by the post-colonial poet. Mahapatra rightly says in a poem called, 1992:

You say you are a poet;
you sit next to me
and talk to me from a distant country.
Yet your own past is too large
for you to talk sensibly about it.

(*Shadow Space* 1997: 14)

In the post-colonial era, the bravery and heroism of the struggle against colonialism during our freedom struggle seems to be missing. This grieves the poet and in a voice marked by anguish and shock, Mahapatra asks:

And I, writing my poem again
What do I remember of faith and past hopes?

and then, he denounces the present generation for failing their ancestors.

Mine was a generation that paid homage
to Gandhi and Tagore, saw in my mother
the State of Dostoyevsky's Grand Inquisitor.
It was the end of the war,

the beginning of the curse of beggardom.
Prophets preached the mysteries of a new kingdom.
Today when I participate in group discussions
or scour the newspapers everyday with urgency,
the words I read and hear
seem simply to walk the globe together,
holding hands and telling stories —
But no truth comes down to the street.
No believer has given up his life for freedom.
There is merely caution in those words,
weak sentiment and history
in which the country's leaders like to drown.

(*Ibidem* 16-17)

Mahapatra is a keen observer of contemporary life and situation and does not mince words in describing socio-political scene that diminishes humanity. Irony becomes his forte. Like a Nissim Ezekiel here and a Derek Walcott there, Mahapatra tries to come to terms with reality. He reminds us of T.S. Eliot in his *The Wasteland* days when the latter spoke of 'the horror and boredom of life, devoid of glory'. Mahapatra is frank and candid in describing the country and the world around him in realistic terms. He 'sees life steadily and sees it whole'. Violence and lawlessness in contemporary society seem to disturb the poet. The disgust of the poet is clearly discernible in a number of poems in his recent works. In a poem titled "Afternoon" (published in *HIMAL* 12/8 August 1999), Mahapatra expresses his disgust and anguish at the rape of girls and women that is reported frequently in the newspapers of our country. He writes:

The harsh afternoon skin of the summer sky
lies in flakes on the dry river bed.
There, the raped and dismembered body
of another thirteen-year old girl, stilled,
beyond the trembling of thc sands.
....
Late afternoon I saw a young widow
strip herself naked by the water.
Just dark bruishes allover her fairbody

made by a world's lust-filled eyes
Kept turning helplessly toward the river

(*Afternoon*)

Mahapatra, is deeply concerned about 'our women's uncertain future', as helpless women get tortured and raped during broad day-light.

As Nationalist writing is the hallmark of post-colonial literature, Mahapatra like his counterparts in African and Caribbean countries focuses on reconstituting from the position of historical, racial difference and tries to gain cultural identity along with socio-political identity which had been affected by colonial experience. Elleke Boehmer makes a point when she underlines this kind colonial experience in the following lines:

Though the nation in certain situations took on wider definitions of race, or of a community identified by its racial oppression, in general the independent nation-state at this time was seen to represent the most achieved form of self-realization for oppressed peoples. Following the incisive analysis of Benedict Anderson, the process of national self-making in story and symbol is often called imagining the nation. What this phrase implies is that the nation as we know it is a thing of social artifice—a symbolic formation rather than a natural essence. It exists in so far as the people who make up the nation have it in mind, or experience it as citizens, soldiers, readers of newspapers, students, and so on. Every new instance of independence, therefore—and some might say each new stage in the process of winning independence—required that the nation be reconstructed in the collective imagination; or that identity be symbolized anew. (1995 : 185)

Jayanta Mahapatra like other leading post-colonial Indian English poets such as Nissim Ezekiel, A.K. Ramanujan, Shiv K. Kumar, R. Parthasarathy and a few others believes that our 'identity be symbolized anew'. The phase of nostalgic harking back to the colonial past is over and Mahapatra has realised the world and felt it in his pulses. Poetry becomes a medium to interpret life and source of sustenance (an extension of Arnoldian vision of poetry that consoles and sustains us) for him. Thus, he makes a bold attempt to depict the reality in this harsh world which engulfs us in a poem called, “The Stories in Poetry”. Mahapatra says,

> The world plots on
> And poetry stumbles and falls
> Everything is called sacred
> in my land. Even poems. And children
> who are sold and bought everyday
> in the streets of Bombay and Calcutta.
> Through words
> I try to recover my balance
> not let life get too far ahead of me. (1997 : 59-60)

As a true post-colonial poet, Mahapatra reflects on the same kind of injustice elsewhere, as he finds in his own country. Discrimination against suffering humanity deeply upsets the poet and disturbs him. Thus, he tells us in the same poem about the hunger in Somalia:

> It’s the world again
> that must not take one unawares
> a world where hundreds die
> of hunger in Somalia and elsewhere —
> where poetry is no mystery;
> even the most tender embrace says
> there is no heroism for us to live on.
>
> (*Shadow Space* 59-60)

Past-coloniality is, as Leela Gandhi says elsewhere, another name for globalization. If the hunger in Somalia disturbs the poet, the undernourished, half-starved children of Kalahandi (a district in his home state of Orissa) make him sad and depressed. The agony abides. Hence, the poet describes the gloomy atmosphere in a matter of fact tone, in a poem titled, “Seeing things in the Dark”.

> Everywhere one looks
> One is stirred by skies
> that protect a bourgeois order,
> and faces goodbyes that suddenly look tired
> before they have been said

Or sees the child-skeleton from Kalahandi
whose neck cannot support
the weight of its head.
Or the death by bullets
that any government calls a natural death.

(*Shadow Space* 72)

The colonial past too haunts him without end and when it is placed by the side of uncertain and disturbed present, adds to the anxiety and worries of the poet. Mahapatra brings alive the past in no uncertain terms in a poem called, "The Absence of Knowledge".

This ground is jagged with the defeat
of races, of morphines of memories;
huge shadows and dark waters of a life time.
now come after us, climbing our way.

(*Shadow Space* 75)

When this past is dovetailed into the present day nuclear world, it adds to our misery.

The poet is concerned with the fate of humanity here in our country as well as in the world. And hence, any form of nuclear weaponry is unacceptable to him. The whole atmosphere is threatened by nuclear holocaust. As he puts it:

The cloud I saw too, bent on suicide
And the underground test, pilgrim of a new world
carrying easily over the distance between us.

(*Shadow Space* 75)

Using 'darkness' as a metaphor for ignorance, which is akin to absence of knowledge, the poet reflects on the colonial past and turbulent present, in a poem called, 'Darkness' (published in *Himal* August 12/8, 1999, p. 49) and asks for a way out.

From a window here and a door there
Darkness lifted its head and looked
who would show it the way?
It slipped past reason and knocked on the Minister's heart
It flaunted its shape, gathering moments
from the light of hostile history

Then came and stood out there
in a middle-class neighbourhood, stark naked.

The 'hostile history' refers to the colonial past, which haunts the post-colonial present. The 'colonial' system and laws are still in operation. We have inherited the British Administrative and judicial system and thereby, kept the umbilical cord intact. This reminds us of his earlier observation, "It is thus the odour of a captured country lingers' ('Life Signs'). Mahapatra is making a whole-hearted effort to decolonise Indian English Poetry. I am inclined to agree with P.P. Raveendran when he says,

"Decolonising poetry, to follow this argument, would mean redefining the limits of the imaginative geography of non-European cultures which, over the past two centuries, have been set to colonial scales of cartography. This is also a recuperation of history by the colonised, as colonialism also has meant for the colonised an effacement of history. This is one reason why scholars like Eric Wolf describe colonised communities as "people without history." Recuperating history therefore, can become a radical act of decolonization accompanied, quite often, by the ex-colonised carving out large territories for themselves within the coloniser's language. Alone of all Indian poets writing in English, with the possible exception of A.K. Ramanujan, it is in Jayanta Mahapatra's poetry that this decolonizing act takes on a quality and specificity comparable to the best verse written in Indian regional languages." (1995: 13)

Mahapatra's knowledge of native language *(i.e.,* Oriya) and inwardness with indigenous tradition and culture are a great help to him in decolonising his poetry. Earlier, he had made experiments with Oriya myths and heroic martial tradition in his Sahitya Akademi Award winning book of verse, *Relationship* to give, as it were 'a local habitation and a name' to his poetry. The landscape of his native place (Oriya in general and Cuttack in particular) coupled with the nuances of speech of the native people, gives a distinct identity to his poetry. Like other post-colonial poets in India, Africa and Caribbean countries, Mahapatra has been busy with reviving the cultural identity that had been damaged by the colonial experience. I concur with Elleke Boehmer when she makes a pertinent point in this regard in the following lines:

"Indian, African and Caribbean nationalist writers focused on reconstituting from the position of their historical, racial or metaphysical difference, a cultural identity which has been damaged by the colonial experience. The need was for roots, origins, founding myths and ancestors, national fore-mothers and fathers: in short, for restorative history." (1995 : 185-86)

This is what Mahapatra does in his poetry. In a recent poem, "Performance" [published in *Poetry Review* 87:2 (London), Summer 1997, p. 26], Mahapatra recalls his father's advice to work hard and likens his fate to a Summer Koel (a singing bird in India belonging to the Cuckoo family). The poet wants to become active and take risks to do human good. He writes:

> But does anything I say or do matter,
> if I risk nothing of my life?
> This easy myth we live in,
> my fate which like a summer koel, answers
> my imitation of its calls through the warm rights.
> Once my father said: If you work hard
> there will be time enough to play later.
> I don't know. If I think of him
> I feel I am staring at the deep water
> of his face with the look of one about to drown.

The use of Indian imagery and introduction of Indian singing birds into the realms of poetry is in the right direction of decolonising Indian English Poetry. Mahapatra has made an effect to evoke a typical Indian atmosphere by describing the Indian sky, landscape, birds and even abandoned temples in his poetry. In our country sometimes some temples are abandoned and rituals are not performed. Then, in some cases the worship resumes after some time. Jayanta Mahapatra describes an abandoned temple in a poem called, "Abandoned Temple", (*Himal,* August 999) and thereby re-creates an actual scene in the following lines:

> A wandering boy hurls a rock through

the ruined entrance. Shadows in retreat fly:
the serpent-girls, elephant-gods, fiery birds.
Mosquitoes slap the Siva linga in ignorant stillness,
a long shiver running down the shrine.

The attempt to build a lively atmosphere out of the surroundings and evoke a sense of 'nativism' is part of the strategy of post-colonial writings. The post-colonial writers seek to describe the indigenous culture and thereby assert their nationality that is both lovable and enduring.

Transnationalism is an important ingredient of Jayanta Mahapatra's poetry. History is being repeated in the perpetuation of violence and cruelty in the present time. The present is not different from the past nor Delhi is any different from Jerusalem and Nicaragua. The poet feels sad to see that the post-colonial era is not much of an improvement on the colonial era—rather it seems to be a continuation of it. Thus, he writes:

Why wait to be free of history
when you are now in it?
Secrets will begin to speak
ashes soak in the rivers.
And the streets
go on enjoying their dead —
either in Jerusalem
or in Delhi or distant Nicaragua.

(*The Waiting* 1997 : 66)

The same theme is reinforced in another poem called 'March'. Like Eliot, Mahapatra seems to say, "people change and smile but the agony abides". Contemporary scene unfolds harsh realities of life and the poet gets disturbed about it. Thus, he writes:

Men here build cities,
cities work their way
into a maze of stories
from where man's mind
fails to see ahead.
The lessons are the same
A story of the future

is not much different
from this game of the past
when Nero heard himself laughing.

(*The Waiting* 81)

One remarkable feature of Mahapatra's poetry is that it integrates the landscape and topography of the place with the mood of the persons who inhabit it as is evident in a recent poem 'Silence' [published in *The Newyorker* (New York) June 23 and 30, 1997]. The inability of the persons to articulate their feelings in the contemporary society is expressed through the seasons of the year. Mahapatra writes:

Rain, all night
capacious, like the body of a woman
And the heat, intolerable.
A cow lows once.

Strong smells of fish and palm-toddy in the air.
One doesn't wish to say anything at all.
How will one crossover? ....

The saints are all silent inside their own truths.
Moss broods silently in the cracks of the stone,
....

Into the moist eyes of the young woman clerk,
returning home,
a herd of shadows has entered
but somehow isn't able to come out

How shall the evening star
give forth its light through the clouds? ....

Your sigh, too, has curled itself up
and lies asleep on a mat in the darkened room.

(*Silence*)

The images are evocative of the mood that the poet seeks to depict in the poem. The voice of the innocent people are being stiffled in an uncongenial atmosphere and hence, the silence. As it is difficult for the evening star to 'give forth its light', so it is difficult for innocent people and children to speak out their mind in a hostile atmosphere. The poet's veiled protest against the contemporary way of life is unmistakable.

In course of an article, "The Decline of Indian English Poetry", published in *The Journal of Indian Writing in English* (Jan. 2000) Mahapatra outlines the role of a poet in the contemporary society.

"Poets are expected to make sense of life. If they find life today in fragments, they must not leave it that way. Perhaps they should have that desire to produce poetry that transcends the ills of modern life rather than poetry that helplessly mirrors them. It is easy for me to say this when I know I am guilty of such writing. But I am afraid this is a difficult task to achieve." *(JIWE,* January, 2000: 4)

This statement is amply borne out in a poem called, "Possessions". Here, he talks about the poets who merely describe their private and public life, and write about the socio-political scene with a sense of empathy. The public expectation of the poets is very high. This is how the poem begins:

> Another day of waiting out, wondering
> about our poets and what they are
> going to say about us.

The realization of the poets' predicament is brought out in an unambiguous note in the following lines:

> In pain perhaps
> they stand inside, but cannot
> yet slam the door of their voice.

Ministers come and go. Wives pretend illness to attend to their ailing husbands. Husbands and wives know that they are lying and yet they don't 'turn their eyes away'. Politicians assume power and make speeches but thousands of children 'go hungry again'. There are many things in the world that happen around us but we do not comprehend them like a little girl who fails to understand "why the wind keeps crying in the telephone wires / and there, how it makes the stars tremble too!" Poetry fails to come to terms with contemporary reality. Thus, the poet says,

Our poems look to the right and to the left,
and then turn to torment in meek expectation
And always the waiting, a hundred years hence
the poems will still be luxurious
hiding their impotent hatred
for the world's unresurrectable life.

Having said this, the poet tries to implore upon the readers that individuals are not very important and what is more, they live not for themselves but for others. The poet asks:

Why is it so hard to realize oneday
that you are meaningless? That one
is not even living for one's own sake?

Individual poets too come and go and are 'silenced by the shapelessness of life alive'. The problems baffle us. The poet asks a rhetorical question:

would the problem disappear
if one puts oneself beyond the judgement of men?
(*Shadow Space,* 1997: 25)

The desire to rebuild the society and reassess life from a new angle underline the message contained in the poem, 'possessions'. Merely telling about life is not enough, one has to face it and live it to the full, the poet seems to say. The optimism expressed in the line, 'There is always a door open somewhere' of this poem, is unmistakable.

If colonial poetry is about the coloniser, post-colonial poetry is in opposition to imperialism and an assertion of the indigenous tradition and culture. Mahapatra applauds 'the native culture showing in the poem of the Indian English poet and quotes a stanza from the northeast poet Robin S. Ngangom ("We heard whatever is not lost/ we speak of a mythic time/let us speak of what we found" *JIWE* Jan. 2000: 6) to say that he likes this kind of poetry—'a poetry that should last'. This is what he also does in his poetry. In order to decolonise his 'self', Mahapatra writes to establish oppositional nationalism as a kind of resistance to the former coloniser. I concur with P.P. Raveendran, when he says:

"Mahapatra's struggle with the colonial self seems to be an ongoing process, and it might be difficult to identify a neat point of rupture between this self and the decolonised self. So that elements connected with the two selves co-exist in his poetry right from the early verse down to the most recent. However, as one moves from *Close the Sky, Ten by Ten* to *A Whiteness of Bone*, one cannot fail to notice a progressive recognition by the poet of the strong need for the former self to yield place to the latter. The native culture has to assert itself in Indian English poetry too." (1995: 14)

Not only that, like Raja Rao doing in Indian English fiction (in *Kanthapura,* to be precise), Mahapatra also tries to create a contemporary myth out of Gandhi in his recent poetry. Gandhi has become a living myth suggesting non-violence, truth and righteousness. Furthermore, Gandhi has also become a synonym for justice and honesty, and passed into Indian mind as an apostle of peace. To deify Gandhi, is part of the process of decolonising the Indian mind and hence, Gandhi becomes an integral part *(i.e.,* a major subject) of post-colonial literature. Mahapatra's recent poem "Excerpts for Requiem" (A poem on Gandhi) published in *JIWE* (Jan. 2000, pp. 7-11) is a case in point. Section XII begins with a statement:

> You became the red earth
> that a perfect, constant gravity
> achieved through the aeons.

and closes with the glorification of ahimsa, Gandhi's principled approach to protest against the unjust persons and injustice in the colonial era, under the British Imperialism:

> It is a world in itself
> this ahimsa,
> with its mysterious shadows
> lurking under ancient places,
> that assumes the clear, self-sustaining light of suns
> a redefinition of beauty

While trying to mythicize Gandhi, Mahapatra realises that one can be authentic as a writer or poet by going back to his/her roots. In his case, he wants to decolonize himself and his culture so that he can be original and authentic, as a poet. In trying 'to be himself', he found his poetry. Thus, he writes:

> And the poem I found at last,
> already lost in the small of the heart,
> just to push the deep, nameless breath
> into the hysterics of history.
>
> (*JIWE* 2000: 8)

Gandhi has become a living legend for us. Even when people disagree with him or his principles, they are conscious of his presence. He has become a part of Indian Psyche. In a fitting tribute to Gandhi, the poet acknowledges Gandhi's unseen presence amongst us, the Indians. Thus, he writes:

> In me
> your body opens slowly
> as if you have been bound tight all your life,
> as if flesh could see
> what the mind believes is true
>
> (*Ibidem:* 10)

The poet comes down heavily on those who wrongly criticise Gandhi and pay only lip service to him. He says,

> Today the voice that points a finger at you
> floats over the breath of discarded ideals,
> the breath of dead flowers day after day at Rajghat...
>
> (*Ibidem*)

And for these misguided people, Gandhi has become a faded picture. With a tinge of irony, Mahapatra writes:

> What you have left behind are
> faded pictures on bare office walls. A day
> every year as a national holiday.
>
> (*Ibidem:* 11)

If creating new national myths is part of post-colonial writing, Jayanta Mahapatra can truly be called a post-colonial poet. He is in the long line of Indian English writers like Mulk Raj Anand, Raja Rao, R.K. Narayan, Chaman Nahal and Nissim Ezekiel who have written eloquently about Gandhi. In fact, Gandhi, himself can be treated as a post-colonial writer because of his oppositional nationalism. (Gandhi and Frantz Fanan are taken as forerunners of post-colonialism by Leela Gandhi in her book, *Post-colonial Theory : Critical Introduction,* 1999).

If we go by Edward Said's prescription that books should be judged 'in terms of their circumstantially or their implication in the social and political imperatives of the world in which they are produced', Jayanta Mahapatra's poetry has little to fear. Said states:

"My position is that texts are worldly, to some degree they are events and even when they appear to deny it, they are nevertheless, a part of the social world, human life, and of course the historical moments in which they are located and interpreted." (1983: 4)

Jayanta Mahapatra's poetry is worldly and full of events. According to Raymond Williams' classification, Mahapatra's poetry is 'indicative' text. Williams brings a distinction between two types of texts—'indicative' text which indicates what is happening in the world and 'subjunctive' text gestures 'towards a radical perspective or impulse which is neither socially or politically available nor for that matter, entirely permissible within the prevailing social order' (Gandhi 1999: 68). In the words of Raymond Williams:

"'Subjunctive' texts are always attempting to lift certain pressures, to push back certain limits; and at the same time, in a fully extended production bearing the full weight of the pressures and limits, in which the simple forms, the simple contents, of mere ideological reproduction can never achieve." (1986: 16)

Mahapatra though wrote some 'subjunctive' texts, he excels in 'indicative' texts. As a humanistic poet, he wrote about what happens around the world. Poems like 'Defeat', 'The Quest', 'Bazaar Scene', 'Heroism', 'the Unease of Quiet Sleep', 'About My Favourite Things' and a few others in his latest book of verse, *Shadow Space* are example of 'indicative' texts. Hence, these poems can be appreciated and analysed better as cultural studies. In 'About my Favourite Things' Mahapatra writes about the drought-stricken Kalahandi (a place that finds a prominent space in Mahapatra's poetry after Cuttack,

Bhubaneswar and Puri) and the sufferings of thousands of people there. He was appalled by the misery that had befallen the people of underdeveloped Kalahandi district of Orissa. The poem is based on the first hand experience of his visit to the place. Thus, he writes:

> Last December, around Christmas
> I felt I should go down the drought-stricken
> Kalahandi countryside and watch my eyes fill with flight
> A tiny straw hut in the fallow fields looked sadly at me.
> It was to keep out the cold, they said,
> the four-by-four frail pyramid of straw
> could easily hold ten men warm
> through the near zero winter nights.
> I went in, lay down
> Caught the odor of sweat and coarse straw.
> Did all earth smell like that?
>
> (*Shadow Space* 49)

Kalahandi is not an exception. In other parts of the world, 'seven hundred miles away' a family were 'burnt to death, simple because/ they had another faith'. The poet is moved by human sufferings at Kalahandi and elsewhere caused by nature or fellow human beings. His heart goes to all the suffering humanity. It is in this aspect that Mahapatra reminds us of T.S. Eliot and nearer at home, Nissim Ezekiel whose heart go for the suffering humanity and who wish mankind well in their later poems. As Mahapatra advances in years, he feels more for the suffering humanity. The things which he could not notice during his youth and middle age, now becomes crystal clear to him and his heart bleeds for humanity. In a poem called 'Defeat', Mahapatra speaks of child labour and the plight of a boy who worked in the blacksmith's shop. Thus, he writes:

> As a child, on my way to school,
> I watched the fire crackle in the blacksmith's shop
> A boy sat smiling, fanning the flames,
> I did not notice his eyes then, misty with pain
> or his hands as he worked with the bellows,
> a finger broken, sores on his thin wrists.

And what is worse is that hunger and suffering go hand in hand. The blacksmith's shop is no more but the suffering of the child labourers has worsened, giving rise to hunger and deprivation. Hence, in a tone full of pathos, the poet records:

> The blacksmith's shop is gone now
> and childhood sits in shadow
> like an eye in a face that is dead
> so the door was opened to hunger and suffering,
> outside, the thick and strange movement
> of human life.

(*Shadow Space* 37)

Poverty, starvation and human suffering go hand in hand. In a poem titled; 'Bazaar Scene', the poet speaks of a three-year old girl child who had stolen a rotten mango from the fruit vendor's basket and given it to her 'crippled brother slumped on the road side.' The plight of the undernourished child and the poverty-stricken mother moved the poet. Thus, with a voice marked by agony the poet asks:

> If the world weeps, are you moved?
> Will it show you where to go?
> Does the world grow according to its own needs?
> Pity is only left for one
> whose eyes are blind to the ways of another.
> With those eyes
> I cannot walk barefoot here.

(*Shadow Space* 23)

Mahapatra is good at cultivating human relationship. One is moved by his concern for fellow poets and love for his contemporaries as is evident in a poem titled "A Day in Marburg on-the-Lahn" (written on the death of A.K. Ramanujan). This is how the poem begins:

> That Summer's day seems suddenly close, you and I
> sitting together in the bus parked beside
> the Elisabethkirche, the others having gone shopping
> up the cute cobbled streets that led
> to the university. Suddenly we were alone
> although it was nothing.

Mahapatra met him twenty years after he had corresponded with Ramanujan. It was a lovely experience for him and he remembers a lot of things that Ramanujan told him that day. They talked freely of poetry they wrote and went for shopping. Ramanujan gave him a bottle of champagne, which Mahapatra brought home *(i.e.,* to Cuttack). He perhaps hoped that Ramanujan would come to Cuttack some day and therefore, he kept the bottle of champagne intact for that day. Mahapatra has told in a seminar *(i.e.,* on March 20, 2000 at Cuttack) that he has not yet opened that bottle. This shows how he wants to preserve his memory of a dead friend and a fellow poet.

The concluding poem, 'March' in *Shadow Space* indicates the mood of the poet who is deeply disturbed by the wanton violence that erupts all around us. The failure on the part of human beings to see the danger that threatens our very existence on earth makes the poet feel sad. As a true humanistic poet, he is disturbed by senseless violence, rape and wanton killings that have become a part of our daily routine life. He writes:

> Men here build cities,
> cities work their way
> into a maze of stories
> from where man's mind
> fails to see ahead ....
>
> and another murder
> of a raped girl on the sea beach
> all these are provisional.

(*Shadow Space* 81)

The concern for humankind and particularly for the poor and suffering people is unmistakable in Mahapatra's poetry. That is why, poem after poem he writes about Nicaragua, Somalia and Kalahandi in order to make the people aware of the contemporary situation. Mahapatra as a poet "sees into the life of things' and makes the reader feel for the suffering humanity. Therein lies his strength and greatness as a poet.

The fifteenth volume of Mahapatra's poetry (*i.e., Shadow Space*) clearly shows that he is one of our best post-colonial poets. The desire to write about an indigenous tradition and culture and establish an identity independent of the coloniser in the recent history, immediately puts him on the forefront of post-colonial poets in our country. Mahapatra's poetry, to borrow a term from Raymond Williams, is largely an 'indicative' text which reflects the contemporary society in its totalitly. To read his poetry is to acquire a kind of empathy with the contemporary life. Mahapatra has successfully decolonized his poetry and made it a vehicle for the expression of Indian scene (both ancient and contemporary) in the post-colonial era. What is more is that he along with other Indian English poets has created a new Indian English idiom (i.e., the other English) that gives 'a local habitation and a name' to post-colonial poetry in our country.

## WORKS CITED

Boehmer, Elleke, *Colonial and Post-colonial Literature*, New York: Oxford University press. 1995.

Gandhi, Leela, *Post-colonial Theory: A Critical Introduction*, Delhi: Oxford University Press 1999.

Mahapatra, Jayanta, "The Decline of Indian English Poetry", *The Journal of Indian Writing in English* (28 : 1, January 2000)3-6.

——, *Shadow Space*, Kottayam; D. C. Books, 1997.

Raveendran, P.P., "Introduction", *The Best of Jayanta Mahapatra*, Calicut: Bodhi Books, 1995.

Said, Edward, *The World, the Text and The Critic*, Harvard University Press, 1983.

Williams, Raymond, "Form of Ficition in 1848". *Literature, Politics and Theory*, Eds. Francis Barker *et al.*, London, 1986.

# Poetry in the Twenty-First Century

7

Jayanta Mahapatra's latest two volumes of poems, *Bare Face* (2000) and *Random Descent* (2005) mark the culmination of his poetic career. There is both continuity as well as break with the earlier books of verse. Contemporary reality which is the hallmark of his poetry continues to pre-occupy the mind of the poet. But the break is seen in terms of creating myths out of the living personalities of the past. Gandhi, for instance, comes to the centre stage of *Bare Face*. This reminds us of W.B. Yeats who created myths out of history. Like Yeats, Mahapatra peopled his poetry with characters drawn from history and contemporary society. To read Mahapatra's latest poetry is to watch the living characters enacting on stage. They are not like Eliot's "shadowy characters" half-guessed, half-understood but full-blooded human beings who love and want to be loved.

In an essay titled "Silence: Poetry's Last Word" included in his latest book of prose, *Door of Paper: Essays and Memoirs* (2007) Mahapatra writes:

> Somewhat hesitatingly, one feels, after years of writing, that one should give up the notion of writing poetry altogether, because this alone is what we know: that they, the words, the makers of poetry, will forever remain beyond us in spite of ourselves and our painstaking attempts to let the poems we have created tell us we would be happy with them, (171).

When words fail, images help as we find in a poem called, "Silence". This is how the poem begins:

Rain, all night,
capacious, like the body of a woman
And the heat, intolerable,
A cow lows once.

(*Bare Face* 13)

Poets like saints take to silence to find their truth. No wonder that the saints are 'silent inside their own truths' and the poets like a garden spider, 'silently spinning its web' choose their words in silence to build their poems.

Like T.S. Eliot, Mahapatra lays emphasis on memory which is associated with rain in a poem titled, "Collaboration".

Father's face is recalled as the poet nostalgically harks back to the past. He negotiates the past with the present through the mango tree. This is how he puts it:

The mango tree my father and I planted
drifts blindly along the monsoon rain,
and air underneath its branches
is deep, cold and clear.
His dead face is poised vaguely somewhere
in the soft talk in the corridor
of my childhood I haven't left behind

(*Bare Face* 15).

If Mahapatra writes about history and time in his early poetry, he seeks to identify himself with the landscape in his later poetry. Poems like "Only Twilight", "In a Time of Winter Rain," and "A Pastoral Perhaps" are cases in point. Twilight touches the heart of the poet as nothing else does. It evokes the past and 'brings in loss, beauty, the nearness of soul'. It is really difficult to perceive how twilight affects your mind and guides your thought. Bewildered by the beauty of it, the poet asks:

Was this twilight simply an idea,
Working it out through the years, from man to man,
An immobility between death and life?

(*Only Twilight*)

In "Traveller", the landscape of the place evokes the suffering of a child who dies in her mother's arms. The poet laments,

"What I'll do with what I learn". The poet feels miserable. Thus, he writes:

> I try to wear this weight lightly.
> But the weight of the unknown buries me,
>
> (*Bare Face* 16)

"In a Time of Winter Rain," memory revives as the poet enjoys the winter rain. The heroic past of Orissa dovetails into the present making the poet conscious of history of his land. The poet asks:

> How I have waited, shaped by memory,
> these many years without knowing exactly why.
> Does childhood spread out all the way
> from the hills of innocence to the horizon of the sea?
>
> (*Bare Face* 18)

Writings about the rocks remind us of the sufferings of young woman as well as the rage of the conquerors of his land.

He writes:

> In the writings on ancient rock, young women
> bound and gagged, etch the grey walls
> with their dead brown bellies, their joyless eyes.
> On the pages of palm leaves they dance, lonelier than ever,
> Stone-bodied courtesans swaying to the dark water.
> Today why does the north wind lack the rage
> of the conquerors of our land?
>
> (*Bare Face* 18)

History and memory are intertwined in "A Pastoral Perhaps". As a woman enters into the village pond to take her bath, shaking her hair the poet imagines the past and re-creates the Indian scene of his childhood days. Thus, the writes:

> The air drops quietly back into the past,
> a part of the present seems to break away.
> The destiny of India heaves in darkness
> in the memory of ancient waters.
>
> (*Bare Face* 27)

"The Return" is a poem that reminds us Mahapatra's Sahitya Akademi Award winning poem, 'Relationship' where Mahapatra recapitulates history only to contrast our present-day rulers with our heroic ancestors. The disappointment stares us in our face. Mahapatra says:

> The sky grown murky
> with promises of leaders unfulfilled.
> And I asked myself: What could embarrass
> our ministers more than people's prayers?
> Rock, altar of my ancestors,
> teach those who rule my impoverished land today
> to stand in your valley of the tortures of the dead
> and feel the shudder that runs down your granite back,
> not revel in the churnings of funereal oceans:
> but remember those unwritten names
> before the falling of the Wall,
> and before the stares of reality
> terrify the child-like blue waters of the Daya,
>
> (*Bare Face* 22)

Like T.S. Eliot and Nissim Ezekiel in the later poetry, Mahapatra too in his later poetry, appeals to us in espousing the cause of suffering humanity. Freedom becomes meaningless for those who live in abject poverty. Thus, in a poem called "Freedom", Mahapatra writes:

> In order for me not to lose face,
> it is necessary for me to be alone.
> Not to meet the woman and her child
> in that remote village in the hills
> who never had even a little rice
> for their one daily meal these fifty years,
>
> (*Bare Face* 34)

Freedom eludes us as we become prisoner of rituals, conventions and lose our way. Thus, says the poet;

> In the new temple man has built nearby,
> the priest is the one who knows freedom,
> while God hides in the dark like an alien.

And each day I keep looking for the light
Shadow find excuses to keep.
Trying to find the only freedom I know,
the freedom of the body when it's alone,

(*Bare Face* 35)

Mahapatra is always against cruelty in any form anywhere. References are made to a Christian missionary who came to Orissa and was burnt to death along with two small children.

In a poem, "For Days Together", the poet hints at the passivity of the people to fight against injustice and words (poetry) too have lost their power to make people see reason. The poet laments:

The days are cold, obsessed by fear.
And the poem's voice is thin, holding
its words of unreason is bizarre arrogance
It's no use taking about my land.

(*Bare Face* 37)

Mahapatra wrote a number of poems on what poetry is and what poetry does in the last two books of verse. Does poetry serve any purpose? Does it begin and end appropriately? Does it fight against injustice? These are some of the questions that disturb the poet. "You have to check whether poetry/really becomes a cry for protecting man", says the poet. On what should he write his poems, becomes a burden for the poet. To use a postcolonial jargan, I should say that if choosing themes for poetry becomes problematic in the present context, negotiating with current issues becomes a pre-occupation for the poet. Thus, Mahapatra writes in "The Lines of My Poem":

This poem stares out ...
It has not been able
to find its way out, ...

(*Bare Face* 43)

The poet does not easily find the way how to compose the poem and what should be theme of it. What will he do? What's his preference? "A screaming, frightened give in Kosovo" or 'generations of man' who, have bled from a terrible history."

Poems bridge the gap between what has happened and what is happening now. Thus, the poet says,

> Poems may run into
> the thunder of their song;
> but the reality of miracles
> doesn't seek out reasons
> for a poem's words:
> the blood doesn't know
> if its fruit is enough
>
> (*Bare Face* 44)

Contemporary life and society give a new opportunity to the poet to use irony as a mode of poetic expression. New images are employed to portray new themes in recent years. In "Postcard from Home," Mahapatra writes:

> In the neighbouring house, a woman hides
> her impotent hatred for her husband.
> And a poet, wrapped in restless shadows
> hurries through the morgue of his words
>
> (*Bare Face* 48)

From individuals, the poet moves to the country and laments its lack of growth even when it moves from plan to plan and government to government. The metaphor used is not the 'light' but shadows to explain the situation. Thus, he puts it:

> Out in the shadows, my country,
> moving from plan to plan,
> from government to government,
> unable to make up its mind
> to light a lamp or do anything sensible
>
> (*Bare Face* 48)

The observation made by the poet of the contemporary life is both authentic and timely. But the irony is implicit.

Allusions to the Australian missionary and his two young sons, who were burnt alive on 22 January, 1999 night are made in the poem, "Progress" with anguish and shock. After that ghastly act what remains is the poem on them that questions again and again the rationale behind this senseless act. Thus, the poet says,

> It was there, friend, this poem,
> its hands folded, eyes shut,
> looking down at those three charred corpses
> of a father and his two young sons
> in the middle of a long journey to nowhere
> what it saw, turned to secret dust,
>
> (*Bare Face* 50)

History is a source of re-enacting the past in the present, as it constantly reminds us of the cruelty done to mankind in the wake of conquest. In a poem called, "Song of Ashokan Edicts, 261 BC", Mahapatra questions the moral lessons written on stones after the Kalinga War. Thus, he writes:

> The letters of morals look unreal,
> As if they've not had their revenge
> for a hundred thousand dead
>
> (*Random Descent* 51)

Against the backdrop of hundred thousand deaths in Kalinga war, the inscriptions written on stone walls after the war, seem to be pointless. A sense of nostalgia takes over the poet. Thus, he writes:

> ... does
> the trembling cry of a cicado on an autumn night
> deaden the chant of ninety-nine monks
> who go on circling these letters on the stone?
>
> (*Random Descent* 51)

Eliot once said, "People may change and smile but the agony abides". Mahapatra seems to endorse this in poem after poem. In "A Growing Ground" Mahapatra refers to the sadness of people far and near who suffer under different circumstances and for different reasons. Be it the sadness of a girl 'whispering with her secret lover', or the sadness of the soldiers, 'who avoid talk about the battles/ in the long letters they need to write home', the poet observes all and asks:

> Does the wound in my side have its place?

Like the nameless black tide
that leaves no trace on the sands,
or the diamonds sparking in Elizabeth's necklace,
and the slow spirals of kitchen smoke
in Orissa's starvation-twilight?

(*Random Descent* 17)

Hunger, is an oft-repeated theme in Mahapatra's poetry. Against the backdrop of hunger caused by famine in Orissa in 1866, the poet's grandfather embraced Christianity at the age of sixteen. This act of his grandfather caused an unhealing wound in the heart of the poet. Thus, he writes:

Memory carries me into strange lands,
my arm around the iron shoulders
of desolate paddy fields.
History, dead river
torments me.
But at times
a worn-out summer left behind
stumbles against the falling skin
of fallow rice fields
as I feel my way
along the defeating distances of hunger

(*Random Descent* 20)

The poet gets disturbed, when he learns that, "Somewhere, inside a room/ a girl is dying in her mother's arms" and expresses surprise, "What I'll do with what I learn". The humanistic touch in a Mahapatra's poetry is unmistakable. Apart from hunger, violence is another reason for the sadness in the heart of the poet, who says, "Senseless Killings hold up their hands to silence me". Violence caused by fundamentalists, greedy people, army and several other people for different reasons creates anguish in the poet's heart. Dowry death is rampant in our country. Mahapatra depicts a situation where dowry death takes place in a poem called "The Uncertainty of Color".

The silent sob from the dying girl
set on fire simply for the color television

she did not bring as part of her dowry
goes around the vow of faithfulness
a vow played
by our game of reward and punishment.

(*Random Descent* 23)

Being oppressed by the realities around him the poet turns inward and seeks to discover his own self and meaning in life. There is as it were a Tagorean quest for unraveling the mysteries of life.

It is through poetry and silence, Mahapatra seeks to relocate himself. Mahapatra writes:

> So, Tagore is a final poem titled *The Unanswered Question* finds himself at a loss for his entire sense of himself and his own work when he asks:
>
> Faced with the emergence of a new being,
> the first day's sun asked.
> "Who are you?"
> There was no answer.

What sort of question was Tagore dealing with when he wrote this? Surely, this was not the manner in which an academic poet today would proceed; there was nothing theoretical here, nothing of theory; simply a subtle attempt toward the painful revelation of a moment of life. I have asked myself often, reading into these lines: what was more alive here, the presence or the illusion? But the answer eludes one (*Door of Paper* 65)

Once again, he refers to Tagore to explain the elusiveness of life. He writes:

> Our very own Rabindranath Tagore wrote some of the briefest lyrics in his later life as he moved toward a silence he could only conceive. Lyrics which were pared and honed to a centre of consciousness as never before, stripped of many of the traditional elements of his earlier style; yet containing that profoundness of thought which makes poetry rise above itself.

On the shore of the western sea
the day's last sun
voiced its last question
in the stillness of dusk.
Who are you?
There was no answer
(Trs. mine)

An enigmatic silence lies behind these lines. Is this what every serious poet moves forward to? Perhaps. It represents a very crucial period in the writer's lifetime (*Door of Paper* 174)

In this context, Mahapatra draws our attention to Edwin Muir statement in the following lines:

> Our minds are possessed by three mysteries: where we came from, where we are going, and since we are not alone, but members of a countless family, how we should live with one another (qtd in *Door of Paper* 71).

Poems like "The Shore", "The Plot" and "Things That Happens", show how Mahapatra's disturbed mind searches for an answer to his existence. He says:

To become myself, it is not possible that
it will be taken away from me, all that I loved.
...
Old sunsets move again in my sky
without amazing me ... with this feeling
that everything has a beginning and an end.

("Things That Happen")

The observation is poignant and apt in "The Shore".

Mahapatra states,

The shore keeps me thinking
why I have come into the world,
one night I stood there as a child
terrified by the almost inaudible beat
of the lovely boat tied to the shore,
the truth was more than I could bear.

(*Random Descent* 75)

The echo of Rabindranath Tagore is unmistakable.

In another poem called "The Plot", the poet is at a loss to comprehend reality and find meaning in life. The poem begins with a note of introspection.

> Today I looked at the bed in my room
> and suddenly thought of a victor standing alone
> in a battlefield with empty hands.
> Like the horizon, any feeling like this
> is always a blur between
> what's real and what's not.
> My life is something else, it is made up of
> silence that say more than was safe for one.
>
> (*Random Descent* 77)

The feeling of not being able to adjust to the new realities of life around him makes him feel depressed. Hence, the anguished cry and loaded question:

> How can I live with the birds who cannot sing and with the wind that had lost its voice starring simply at those fabulous, holy oil lamps that perform their ritual in a musty despths of life?
>
> (*Random Descent* 77)

For Mahapatra, unlike Wordsworth, feeling comes through writing—not vice-versa. In course of an article, "Containing the World that contains us: Myth/Symbol as Metaphor in Poetry", Mahapatra states it clearly:

By the very act of writing the poem, the poet is learning to feel himself. When I am reading someone else's writing, then my own response to the work may be broadly speaking of two kinds—original and fresh and sincere, or derivative, cliched and insincere. Probably my reaction, my conviction to the poem's sincerity would build from the thought or the ideas of the poem, which the poet finds out not through spontaneity or what we might call inspiration (a terrible enough word)—but through a process of careful thinking, which means again a scrupulous and exact weighing of the words the poet makes before they are finally incorporated into the poem.

And so the poet learns how to feel by writing the poem.
(*The Door of Paper* 183-184)

Such a feeling for art is expressed in a poem called, "Madhuri Dixit". Madhuri's dance eludes the poet who seeks to put her in the Indian mythical tradition. The poet calls it a 'poem of the soul'. For him, Madhuri in her dance combines the past and the present, the real and the mythical and above all life and art. Hence, he says,

How would I know you are river and waterfall,
a story of the tide playing with abandon
in the five estuaries of the Indian dream?
It is a pity you cannot see what we see;
that in you is the eternal, and over you
the world keeps on moving, as it has before –
perhaps Radha, perhaps Menaka, determining
the limits of India's prodigal imagination;
your womb in happiness, shame and pain
is a truth we will not understand.
(*Random Descent* 35)

I would like to end this chapter with a reference to a poem, (which I consider to be utterly personal) called, "Predicament". This stands as a contrast to A.K. Ramanujan's Poem, "Small Scale Reflections on a Great House". The poem is addressed to the poet's wife, Runu, who died on 14 May, 2008 (of course, she was alive when the poem was written and published). The feelings expressed in the poem are heartfelt and genuine and therefore, it touches the heart of the 'Sahridaya Pathak' (the ideal reader). The poem begins with a matter of fact tone and candid statement:

Dear Runu, everything moves here
but nothing really comes.
The children play their games
but they belong somewhere else
In the mirror the mirage stays:
the sky, the street, the park.
The branches ache, heavy with fruit
the birds vanish, ageing with silence

But as always nothing comes

(*Random Descent* 49)

When blood relations and one's children move away, they create a wound in the heart which never heals. Such a wound is there in the heart of the poet, who closes the poem with a heavy heart.

There is just the lonely mirror
feeding on life, on shadows of the past.
And absence is like a child's puzzle
abandoned to an indifferent adult world.

(*Random Descent* 49)

*Bare Face* and *Random Descent* reveal a new dimension of Mahapatra as a contemporary Indian English poet. That is, the note of humanism is unmistakable. Head and heart go together as the poet realizes that, 'I am never anything but myself.' No wonder, he expresses sympathy with those who have been victimized by cruelty in contemporary society. If history, and myth dominated his best known poem, *Relationship*, geography, and contemporary reality become the bedrock of his latest poetry. The poet does not run away from reality and states firmly that "I accept what I see through the open window / and between its rigid iron bars". The sadness of suffering humanity moves the poet as he looks at the happenings around him. He finds no answer to human suffering and accepts it as an integral part of life. The places and people mentioned in his latest poetry are real—only the names have been changed. The real strength of his latest poetry lies in making people realise the plight of others and invoking a sense of empathy with the suffering humanity. In his latest poetry, he comes closer to Nissim Ezekiel who wanted to do some 'human good'.

## WORKS CITED

Mahapatra, Jayanta. *Bare Face*, Kottayam: D.C. Books, December 2000.

——*Random Descent*, Bhubaneswar: Third Eye Communications, 2005.

——*Door of Paper: Essays and Memoirs*, Delhi: Authors Press, 2007.

# Conclusion

# 8

JAYANTA MAHAPATRA is one of the most well known and talented Indian English poets of our time to whom the younger poets turn to for inspiration and perhaps, guidance. In this concluding chapter, I wish to make an assessment of the achievement of Jayanta Mahapatra as an Indian English poet and his contribution to Indian English poetry.

Critics have lebelled him variously: both as a modernist and a post-modernist poet. Bruce King, a well-known foreign critic makes an interesting observation:

"By contrast to Mehrotra's verse constructions, Jayanta Mahapatra seems closer to the modernist movement of the first half of this century with its open-ended literary forms and reliance on recurring symbols to provide coherence to non-linear, fragmented structures. Mahapatra's persona is an estranged, distanced, sensitive artist rather than an invisible or playfully prominent post-modernist author. As in modernist writers there is less importance on the material world and more emphasis on subjective memory and the innerself, the psychological, in contrast to the post-modernist's emphasis on almost totally self-enclosed art forms. Mahapatra's is an elite art, aimed at a small discriminating readership—whereas the early Mehrotra's humour was iconoclastic and his anti-art position had populist tendencies, common to some post-modernists who have turned to popular culture or contentless writing in reaction to high culture. But while Mehrotra's style is post-modern he has none of the sense of life as an endless repetition, an unchangeable chain found in some of the present day avantgarde, Mahapatra's vision and obsessive writing of poetry as hopeless search for meaning in the human condition is, however, a characteristic of post-modernism as found in Beckett's later work."[1]

John Oliver Perry is of the opinion that, 'In trying to place and understand his achievement, we might assume, as many critics in India have done, that if an Indo-English poet like Mahapatra must work in the absence of any appropriately hyphenated—that is, culturally mixed yet indigenous—tradition, his only alternative is to adopt some type or other of the Anglo-American modernist, avant-garde or post-modernist styles as 'tradition' or otherwise seek something similar among the current international, exile or dissident models."[2] Like A.K. Ramanujan, R. Parthasarathy, Arun Kolatkar and Kamala Das, Jayanta Mahapatra turns inward to get into his roots. He feels the need for acclimatizing English language to an indigenous tradition (in his case, Oriya tradition) to write poetry effectively. It seems natural that a poet with a live cultural past behind him, aware of his roots and perhaps prejudiced by those roots, has greater probability of writing significantly than one who has no knowledge of any Indian language other than English. Mahapatra's *Relationship* is set in Orissa - a land of 'forbidding myth'. He is 'caught in the currents of time' and in his attempt to 'go into the unknown in me', tries 'to speak of the myth of sleep and action', in order to soothe himself and others who suffer a similar fate.

As a modern poet he tries 'to connect' a man with the contemporary world and searches for an identity that is both lovable and enduring. Mahapatra writes:

"In a poem I wrote about fifteen years ago and which was first published in 'Poetry' I found myself once again at the border between two separate regions of mind—between what perhaps, I understood and what I did not, using 'rain' as a symbol for that substance which makes up my life, those blurs of vague light that pulsate with the days, making me ask at the end of the poem:

> Which still, stale air sits on an angel's wings?
> What holds my rain so it's hard to overcome?

To-day, the same questions bother me although I see no specific cause or rationale for such things. But such searching moves me, and I am unable to resist it in my poetry. For poetry is voice—'Vaak'—and it is a voice forged from those elements which constitute the world both within and without: a voice which carries with it its unusual power of survival."[3]

In Mahapatra's poetry, one discerns both the ways 'the voyage within' and 'the voyage without' - in one he tries to evoke a native tradition and acclimatize it to English language and in another to make poetry out of contemporary life. And it is to his credit that he excels both ways. As John Oliver Perry has rightly observed:

"Social reports are infrequent in Mahapatra's work after *A Father's Hours* (1976), we cannot expect him to explain India to us—whatever that huge and varied political entity is. Rather, we find, as in modern poems generally, some searching understanding of one man's feelings about his inner world, highly imagistic meditations set frequently in natural scenes - by rivers, in fields, under bird-filled, wide open or more often rain-drenched, monsoon skies. Often rejected by editors who comment on their being 'overtly philosophical' his poems brood darkly, coming to very uneasy terms with questions imposed by his world and his karmic sense of guilty involvement in it. The scenes, being Indian, often have social dimensions (for example, a temple, a street, a decayed fort) but if other people are present, there is no interaction with this slowly communing, inturned gaze. As if to minimize local reference for non-Oriyan readers, only occasionally are the settings for these meditations, or even their flora and fauna, specifically named. Several occur on the banks of the Mahanadi ('Big River' at Cuttack). Two are titled *The Captive Air of Chandipur on Sea* and *The Abandoned British Cemetery at Balasore* and he often alludes to nearby temples at Puri and Bhubaneswar and Konarka, the locus of his favourite poem, *Relationship* and presumably for his other, never, long poem, *Temple*, excerpted here. With extended attention, the interiority feels profoundly localized and alive with Hindu and other social and historical pressures from the ancient and recent British past, all still very pressing in immediate experience."[4]

*Relationship* combines within it history, myth and vision. It is set in a land of 'forbidding myth' - *i.e.* Orissa. Jayanta Mahapatra does the same thing in *Relationship* as R. Parthasarathy did in *Rough Passage* in trying to acclimatizing English language to an indigenous tradition. The myth of twelve hundred artisans working day and night to complete the Konarka temple under the authority of a 'ruthless emperor' has evoked sympathy in our hearts. From the building of Konarka temple Mahapatra takes us down the memory lane to our 'maritime ancestors' who brought glory to the State. Time has withered away everything but the racial memory haunts the poet without end. The Mahanadi, Konarka and 'maritime' ancestors remind the poet of a glorious past of the land of his birth and thus he ends the first section of *Relationship* with a sense of belonging:

> Only that the stones were my own,
> waiting as mother or goddess or witch,
> as my birth feeds on them
> as though the empty dugs of sorcerous thought.

The heroic past is vividly remembered and recalled with great despair. The 'guilt consciousness' haunts him without end when the realisation is drawn upon him that his generation has not been able to keep up the martial tradition of his ancestors. The glory and pride of our ancestors exhibited in the climactic Kalinga war in 261 B.C. which changed the Emperor Ashok, the Great from a despotic monarch to a deeply religiousman are things of the past. The river Daya is a silent witness to our ancestors' heroic act all through the ages. Thus, the poet writes:

> Orion Crawls like a spider in the sky
> while the swords of forgotten kings
> rust slowly in the museum of our guilt.

The poet is at a loss to understand how the successors of such great ancestors have become so unheroic and unworthy of their predecessors. An awareness of contemporary situation brings the poet to the realm of history of our land right from the time

Lord Buddha sat in meditation 'under the peepal tree'. Then he traces his own birth at Cuttack where numerous gods and goddesses are worshipped. Cuttack, a city of historical importance which had the great Barabati Fort is now a symbol of 'vanquished dynasties'. The past is brought alive for a moment, 'of broken empires and of vanquished dynasties/and of ahimsa whimpers'. The poet now standing among the ruins drifts through his weariness, listening to the voices of his friends and 'writing poems', 'with the smells of the rancid fat of the past'.

Mahapatra is aware of the changing contours of contemporary life and makes poems out of it. He states his position clearly in the following extracts:

"My themes in my poems have changed, some of them I am keenly aware of the world I live in today; the mournful bleating of goats as they are led to the municipal slaughter house in my town every morning awakens me. There seems to be debris everywhere; over the deep blue sea, across the broken grain in the fields of India, in the answers to questions our children do not need any more."[5]

"The point is: I wanted to make sense of the life which lay in fragments before me, I was urged to seek answers of myself, testing my feelings by striking them against the fabric of the poem I knew I must write."[6]

"Today, I would say that my poetry suffers from such endless questioning, and also from the cliched subjects of time, death and the quest which man is after; but such thoughts come out from the meditation on the immediate landscape of my mind... It therefore, becomes a natural consequence of the writing of poetry that it should proceed toward a clearer definition of humanity. Maybe to achieve this, the poet tries to redefine his reality in his own terms."[7]

*The Lost Children of America* is a bright example of how Mahapatra makes poems out of contemporary situation.

> I have no need to ask
> why they come ten thousand miles
> for though their eyes are open they

appear asleep,
and perhaps they too are men with
dreams:
these men rushing through endless
super market aisles!
appearing like lost children who
wamder bare-eyed
smelling of incense and living on
grass and flowers.

In *A Whiteness of Bone* a number of poems grew out of contemporary situation and remind us of the everyday reality that engulf us. Such poems are "The Waiting", "The Fifteenth of August", "Of Independence Day", and "Red Roses for Gandhi". The outbreak of violence all over the country makes the poet depressed and the irony is that we have now learnt to live with it. Mahapatra writes:

And the streets will go on
enjoying their dead—whether in Jerusalem,
in Delhi or in far-off Nicaragua.
I can easily tell the sound
of someone being hit with an iron pipe
the sound of a body falling
or being burnt after being doused in petrol
and the sound of someone reducing my woman
these are like the sun and air
on my face now.

(*The Waiting*)[8]

Mahapatra's pre-occuption with the naked earth of which Orissa forms a significant part—the favourite places such as Jagannath Puri, Cuttack, Bhubaneswar, dominates his thought and helps him to search for his 'self'. There is, as it were, a total identification of the man with his environment, the earth that raised him and this approach brings Mahapatra closer to other leading commonwealth poets. The pre-occupation with the 'image' of the native land and a search for identity in terms of 'self' are predominant traits with commonwealth poets. Mahapatra, is not only an Indian English poet but a leading commonwealth poet as well. His attempts to relate his life to his land of birth, may be taken as an exploration of the 'self':

> I try to pull back my life
> as if from a great distance.
> Crowds beyond my life look up
> expecting it to reveal my true identity.
>
> [*The False Start* (1980)]

As a bilingual writer, Jayanta Mahapatra faces certain problems while writing poetry in English. He is conscious of the fact that he is writing poetry in a second language, though he calls it a foreign language ( I do not subscribe to the view that English is a 'foreign language' or an 'alien language' to us for it has been with us for nearly two hundred years. Moreover, English being our medium of instruction at the college level, can be appropriately called 'a second language' in our situation. For Mahapatra, English was the medium of instruction from his school days). He has the courage of conviction to write poetry in English, come what may. Thus he writes:

> Yes, there's a poem growing
> with a foreign language which keeps my head up;
> I don't try to explain
> whether it's the right thing to do or wrong,
>
> (*Even If No One Takes My Poems Seriously*)

No Indian English poet has yet evolved a theory of his own. However, some of them are aware of process which facilitates the making of a poem. Jayanta Mahapatra has his own notion of what poetry is and does. Let us examine his views on poetry which provide a clue to the understanding and appreciation of his own poetry. In course of an article titled "The Inaudible Resonance in English Poetry in India", published in *The Literary Criterion* Mahapatra explains how a poet, ' 'begins to be drawn into an inner world of his own making—a world spaced by his own life, of secret allusions, of desire and agony, of a constantly changing alignment between dream and reality."[9] He goes on to say that, 'as I grope from poem to poem for the key to human understanding, at times it becomes painfully obvious that the bits and pieces of the nature of existence which

I give place to in a poem, have become incapable of integration, incapable of coalescing into a haunting whole."[10] This kind of idea prompts the poet to take an inward turn, to look within and perhaps to turn to silence. Here he comes closer to Nissim Ezekiel's view when the latter emphasizes to 'turn to silence, nothingness' to write poetry effectively. A sense of mystery haunts the poet when he is absorbed in the process of poetic creation. Mahapatra makes it clear in course of another article titled, "The Measure of Mystery in Poetry" published in the *Journal of Literary Studies*:

"So for me a poem is knit together by an inconceivable silence. Silence which is intangible substance, of which words are but manifestations, words which can build the poem from a silence and to which the poem must eventually return."[11]

Poetry for Mahapatra is a craft which needs to be chiselled. Like Eliot and Yeats abroad and Ezekiel at home, he believes in revising a poem. Like Eliot measuring life with coffee spoons, Mahapatra measures the silence in his poetry "with symbols like 'rain' or 'sleep' or 'stone' once again, which are very private symbols."[12] Since poetry makes use of private symbols and is imbued with a sense elusiveness, the poetic process is bound to be a mystery. Mahapatra's poetry appears to be complex because of its language and allusiveness. It is never plain as one finds in the poetry of a Kamala Das or an Ezekiel. His poetry is a dialectic of the personal and the impersonal. I am inclined to agree with S.K. Desai's observations on Mahpatra's poetry:

"His poetry is essentially poetry of exploration, but what he explores is often a not very important mood in the context of some object or a natural phenomenon or a historical religious place. Although there is a certain maturity of perception, what is certainly admirable is his Keatsian readiness to live with uncertainties. There is no Eliotian or Yeatsian movement towards a vision or a revision. There is only an interesting flow of poetic consciousness which is all inclusive and apparently pointless in its ethical and philosophical openness."[13]

Mahapatra's poetry gets its strength from the juxtaposition of the concrete and the abstract and of the expected and the unexpected in the manner of the English Metaphysicals. One gets an example of 'a unified sensibility' in his poetry. His is an authentic voice whose mastery over the medium commensurate with the vision behind it. He has come to terms with himself and discovered his own voice. Critics like Alan Kennedy and Norman Simms view Mahapatra not as a modern poet but a post-modern poet. Hence, his method of writing becomes important as it helps us to approach and appreciate his poetry. Latest critical method like Deconstructionism might help in examining his poetry. Thus, Alan Kennedy writes:

"Mahapatra's poetry then is an errant confrontation with writing itself: It wanders into words and into strange possibilities of meaning. It is a method, the method of language itself functioning by means of chains of signifiers, which reveal themselves as belonging to a chain only after they have been manifested in one. Thus, the signifiers: rain, flutter, feet, earth, wings, summer, dream, escape, face, code, crickets, dying, habit, art belong to a signifying chain produced by Mahapatra's method."[14]

The assessment of Jayanta Mahapatra's poetry will not be objective and convincing unless one takes into account his own views of poetry along with the poets who have influenced him. His growth and development depend on how he extricates himself from the spell of the poets and discovers his own voice. Mahapatra who began his poetic career by echoing T.S. Eliot and Nissim Ezekiel [his first book, *Close the Sky, Ten by Ten* (1968) began with quotations from both Eliot and Ezekiel], has grown in stature over the years. Like R. Parthasarathy, Mahapatra, who was lured by the charm of English language in the beginning has understood the art of writing poetry in the second language. The process of writing became a kind of self-exploration and self-discovery for him. Thus he writes:

"I started writing poetry late... When I began, I suppose I was more carried away by what the English language could do; I was so much obsessed by the feel for words, their sound qualities. It was a wrong thing perhaps, this craze for language, and hence my first poems were in a way attempts in which the language left the ideas of the poems behind them, lost in the depths of words. But as the years went by and I went on to publish more, finding out what my contemporaries in other countries were writing, my notions of poetry kept changing. Today I see that the idea behind the poem (or in the poem) is slowly beginning to surface, and my poems are perhaps being more direct ones. But I am in no position to talk about my poems. The poems, the poetry remain exploratory, as I try to find out the person within myself, as I try to face this stranger that comes out of my poetry."[15]

An introspective study of the 'self' gives Mahapatra a new direction and a kind of authenticity that immediately sets him apart from many other contemporary Indian English poets and brings him to the company of a Nissim Ezekiel, and a R. Parthasarathy. As he puts it:

"You say that my poems are a sort of private ritual of discovery, relationship and reaching out to others, if there is a catharsis in my writing, it comes about involuntarily if there is a spiralling as I try to get into the centre of myself, I feel I am somehow afraid of this closeness too, and I try to move out from the centre of my life. Yes, my poetry might be a ritual of finding myself first, feeling the beat of the blood in my hand which feeds only myself."[16]

Though Mahapatra denies any lasting influence on his work, he too acknowledges that he is fond of some poets who strike him and he benefits from them. Thus, he states.

"I am more fond of the European and Latin American poets today than the American poets, for example. But I admire Robert Penn Warren, especially his later books... I enjoy reading Neruda, Seferis, the Spanish poets Alexandre, Alberti, Cernuda and Jiminez."[17]

Mahapatra is aware of the changing contour of his poetry with the passage of time. Being a conscious artist, he 'looks before and after' and pines for what it is not. He is forthright in his answer with reference to the state of his poetry now.

"Today, I would say that my poetry suffers from such endless questioning, and also from the cliched subjects of time, death and the quest which man is after, but such thoughts come out from the meditation on the immediate landscape of my land. I am struck by the poetry of Allen Ginsberg, a poet who has probably lived closer to the limits of the history of his time than any other poet in America."[18]

Jayanta Mahapatra began his poetic career with enthusiasm but his fascination for English language soon gave way to a kind of pessimism when he encountered the problem of expressing himself in a second language with which he had no inwardness. The same problem was earlier highlighted by R. Parthasarathy in a subtle way, 'My Tongue in English Chains', as he put it. But unlike Parthasarathy, Mahapatra did not think of returning to his mother tongue for creative expression (Parthasarathy too continues to write poetry in English). Mahapatra explained in an 'Inner View' for the premier *Tenor* (June 1978) in course of a conversation with N. Raghavan:

"I am not a born poet. When I finish a poem, I do not know how to begin the next one. It is a great strain .... (In India) we miss the slang of common usage, and come out eventually with an opaque language. You could say there is a frigidity in the language we use ... But that should not deter us ..."

In our country the Indian English writers face the problem of communication in a language which is not the language of the masses. That is why there is an attempt to create a new idiom (namely the Indian English idiom), as the vehicle of their expression. Raja Rao raised the problem way back in 1938 in his introduction to *Kanthapura.* Indian English poets like Nissim Ezekiel, P. Lal, R. Parthasarathy, Kamala Das, Jayanta Mahapatra and a host of other poets are aware of this problem. But they have taken the problem of communication in English in their stride and made an attempt to recreate the characters in their own situation. The *Poetry of Popular Impersonation* (G.S. Fraser's Coinage) brings the incidents, characters and situation alive before the readers and gives a sense of immediacy to Indian English poetry. Jayanta Mahapatra has tried to catch the nuances of Indian English and succeeded to a great extent in conveying the 'feel' of his poetry in a 'live idiom'. I would like to return to the point made by Bruce King when he described the poetry of Mahapatra as closer to the Modernist movement while his style is post-modern. Let us first examine, What is 'Modernism?' and then, what should we call Mahapatra—a modern or a post-modern poet? *Oxford English Dictionary* defines modernism as 'A usage, mode of expression, or peculiarity of style or workmanship, characteristic of Modern times'. G.S. Fraser in his *The Modern Writer and His World* speaks of "an imaginative awareness of the stress of social change."[19] In an introduction to *Mapping Literary Modernism: Time and Development,* R.J. Quinones writes:

"As a literary movement and broad cultural force, Modernism has made its mark and has had its impact. It has entered into history and needs now to be discussed with the same comprehensive scope and yet with the same historical imagination that we might muster in discussing the Renaissance or Romanticism. Certainly the time is long part when distinguished literary historian (who here shall be nameless) could refer to the use of the term 'modernism' as pretentious. Modernism has become, in that celebrated Modernist Phase, 'a climate of opinion', and now permeates the every day life and common patois of the time, it being with us when we knew it not."[20]

Two well-known critics in America in post-War II period, Harry Levin and Lionel Trilling have opined clearly that Modernism is a literary movement, though they differed from one another on the basic purposes as well as the origins of Modernism. "Trilling, from *The Liberal Imagination* onward, has emphasized the Modernist insight into the more irrational sides of human experience, thus associating modernism, in what we call its first phase, with the theories of Nietzsche and German Philosophy. Levin on the other hand, has underscored the consciousness of Modernism with its roots in the Enlightenment. His version of Modernism suits well with the great classic of the twenties."[21]

Modernism as a literary movement and cultural force came to India only after the Indian Independence much after it brought about a change in the west and perhaps paved the way for post-modernism. In the field of Indian English poetry P. Lal and K. Raghavendra Rao ushered in a new era by bringing out their anthology titled, *Modern Indo-Anglian Poetry* in 1959. P. Lal discarded the poetry of the earlier generation—particularly the poetry of Sri Aurobindo and Sarojini Naidu for its vague poeticism and idealism. Prof. Lal prefers concrete ideas, images to abstract thought and states:

"We think that poetry must deal in concrete terms with concrete experience. That experience may be intellectual or emotional or historical-tragical-pastoral-comical, but it must be precise and lucidly and tangibly expressed. It is better to suggest a sky by referring to a circling eagle in it than to say simply 'the wide and open sky'."[22] If Modernism means a transformation of 'self' then the discovery of a shaping spirit in the 'self' amounts to a pattern of vindication and "is the basis of hopefulness in Modernist writers. In Stephen's Aristotelian language this is the 'entelechy', the basic form whose potential is being realised in time. It persists through multiplicity, and even multiple selves, and emerges to predominate and give legitimacy to the activities of the individual. Along with the context of ordinariness and the remarkably consistent factor of involuntariness, the discovery of the self is the distinguishing feature of this new phase of Modernism"[23] , and in the poetry of Jayanta Mahapatra this 'self' is projected onto the larger screens of history and of myth. No doubt, Mahapatra has depicted the contemporary life with rare insight and vividness. He too evoked the myth of the land and tried successfully to acclimatize an indigenous tradition to English language. His two long poem 'Relationship' and 'Temple' are cases in point.

A newspaper report on the death of an octogenarian couple belonging to the Weavers' Community forms the background of the poem, 'Temple' and it ends with another newspaper report on the death of a twelve year old girl allegedly gang raped and murdered. The poem ends where it begins. Through the character of Chelammal, the poet seeks the identity of a woman under the preconscious system of beliefs and values associated with the concepts of 'moksha', 'dharma' which is a materiality for Hindus.[24]According to the Hindu concept the 'self' is a continuation from the earlier life and it can be projected into the physical body of someone else. The Putana myth explains how a woman can enter into another body and elude others for some time till she returns to her own 'self'. The transformation of 'self' is unique that explains the Hindu doctrine of 'moksha', 'dharma' and 'karma'. Mahapatra shows how such a myth enacts in the life of Chelammal:

> Around the kingdom of Opals she wandered
> making her need be led by the words of her myth
> crossing world upon world, breaking vision upon vision
> moving about in circles of timeless power
> ... ... ... ... ... ...
> ... ... ... ... ... ...
> and she forgot who she was —
> she was already a stranger
> making to the rhyapsodic incantation of memory,
> disturbed in the silences of mythic streams,
> in a self-possessed past of safe voices and lipless noises
> through a wind plucking the peaceful rests from her breast
> through chains of history shining between the eyes of Karma
> (*Temple,* pp. 46-7)

As Putana transformed herself into a lovely woman to poison the child, Lord Krishna, Chelammal may transform herself into another woman and may evade the evil part of the 'self'. Thus the poet says,

> And now the ogress,
> transformed into a lovely woman,
> her poisoned nipples
> the moksha—centre of her own martyrdom.
> awakens the woman of the mind
> seeking the light in hidden knolls
> where the red hearts of rocks
> stop beating
> when the year's hysterical winds pass by.

To know one's self is not egoism but the gateway to all virtue. The Putana myth which is the core of the poem, 'Temple' makes us aware of the transformation of the 'self' and paradoxically this ancient myth explains the multifacetedness of 'self' in the modern world. It is in this sense that one woman is not one but many and all women are at last one woman.

The attempt to define myth seems to be far from easy and the poet moves from myth to contemporary life to learn the anguish and predicament of modern man. In 'Relationship' he traces his own birth at Cuttack where numerous gods and goddesses are worshipped. Cuttack, a city of historical importance which had the great Barabati Fort is now a symbol of 'vanquished dynasties'. The past is brought alive for a moment, 'of broken empires' and of 'vanquished dynasties', and of 'ahimsa whimpers'. There is as it were, a nostalgic harking back to the past and a sense of belonging overwhelms the poet.

> Now I stand among the ruins,
> waiting for the cry of a night bird
> from the river's farside
> to drift through my weariness,
> listening to the voices of my friends....
> with the smells of the rancid fat of the past.
>
> (*Relationship*)

The poet now standing among these ruins drifts through his weariness, listening to the voices of his friends and 'writing poems' with the smells of 'the rancid fat of the past'. The present would be better understood, appreciated and endured in the light of the past and one would learn how to live from other people's lives. Mahapatra's conception of man's relation to what he perceives brings him face to face with history and myth when his 'self' is discovered in the 'act of attention' (Lawrence's phrase). The interaction between 'self and reality—the reality that eludes but includes man, form the bedrock of Mahapatra's poetry. Poetry for him is the explorations of the myths and it is linked with the world of art and sculpture. Hence he continues his quest for 'an essence divine' and for 'grace' in relationship between man and man, man and god, and god, man and sculptured art.

It goes without saying that Jayanta Mahapatra is closer to the modernist movement that swept the first half of our century. Some trait of his poetry is also closer to the post-modernist movement. I believe, that it would be very apt to call Mahapatra a contemporary Indian English poet or more specifically a post-1970 Indian English poet, who though closer to both modernist and post-modernist movement of the west in our country does not belong to either. One would do well to remember that 'Modernist' movement in the west was very short-lived as 'Post-Modernist' movement immediately followed it in quick succession. Harry Levin's essay, 'What was Modernism?' (1960) clearly indicates that 'Modernism" has already yielded place to 'post-modernism' by 1960. R.J. Quinones clearly states about these two movements in the following manner:

'At the 1976 meeting of the Modern Language Association of America, no less than six sessions were directly devoted to questions of Modernism, but at the 1979 meeting nine sessions had postmodernism as their subject. These meetings revealed a need: One—had the impression that the speakers were talking through one another (although this is perhaps the nature of such meetings), and that the issues had not been profitably joined. It was almost as if, in this time of rapid change, Modernism had been passed by before it had been fully understood."[25]

Apart from the shift from 'Modernism' to 'Post-Modernism' in the west within a very short period, in India these terms cannot be used appropriately for here, the values are tradition bound. I am in agreement with John Oliver Perry when he makes the following observations:

"A poetry authentically relating to the here and now is necessarily poetry both aware of changes from the past and projecting some personal or social vision ahead—and that is surely all that a modernistic poetic initiative need involve, it is certainly not 'experiment' for the sake of 'distinction'. To this extent then, modern poetry in English can serve in India the special function that its cultural and historical position requires to give substance and shape to all the tensions—the harrowing ones and the pleasing the inevitable and the chosen—that mark everyday life and special moments and places."[26]

Jayanta Mahapatra's poetry takes the past into its orbit infuses it with the present and looks forward to the future. It at once encompasses the history, the myths and embodies a vision for the future. Hence, it defies the exact terminology 'modern' and 'post-modern', for it is imbued with the sense of contemporaneity that includes both 'Modernism' and 'Post-Modernism'. In literature Post-Modernism is associated with Post-Structuralism, which emphasizes the indeterminancy of meaning. The deconstructionists have taken an extreme position by saying that the text has deconstructed itself. Hence the Post-Structuralists, say that there is no reading but only misreading and no understanding but only misunderstanding. And finally, there is no text but only sub-texts. Paradoxically, both modernism and post-modernism share the common feature indeterminancy, in meaning between them. In his pre-occupation with self and in his attempt to go beyond it Mahapatra shares some of the characteristics of both Modernism and Post-modernism. The later poetry of Mahapatra may seem to us as Post-modernist in both its relaxation of form and its semantic indeterminancy. Even some of his poems defy interpretation because of semantic incompatibility, which can be explained only by creative deviation and foregrounding.

However, Mahapatra can be understood and appreciated better if viewed against the Indian, not the Western background. His attempt to speak of the myth of sleep and action, in the hope of 'soothing myself and those others' in order to recreate the past in the present context by re-enacting the myth reminds us of W.B. Yeats' 'Myself must I remake' and T.S. Eliot's 'Shall I at least set my lands in order?' That is how, a great artist obtains the tradition with great labour and enriches it with his individual talent. To my mind, Mahapatra has been successful to a great extent in bringing a native tradition alive in his poetry. In an article titled, "The Decline of Indian English Poetry" published recently in *The Journal of Indian Writing in English* (January 2000) Mahapatra laments the decline standard of recent Indian English poetry for it 'does not touch us in our deepest, most enduring 'self' and what is worse, it is lacking in ideas. He suggests a remedy for post-colonial poetry *(i.e.,* post-Independence Indian English Poetry).

"I believe our poetry will not be noticed until we explore our writing within the context of a unifying outlook on life. It is easy to make poems that are urged by sporadic, individual responses to things—to write a poem on the potato I mentioned earlier, but perhaps to seek an insight into the potato's mind haunted by the sinister density of the earth. Perhaps we never try to seek that experience and perception that make up for what we call the poet's "vision," I do not know how to define these things. But this way of going into the meaning of the insight is more likely to be achieved slowly as a result of simply living and responding to things in the world, of reading and thinking, and in the daily work of writing poems.

Every poet seeks to accomplish like this in the poems he writes, or else he would not be able to write at all. But he or she should not forget his or her own roots even though the work is written in English. One of the strengths of poetry in Spanish in our time is that it has not lost contact with the past. Quevedo and Gongora are still living presences for poets in Spain and South America, as they were for Lorca and others of his generation.

It wouldn't be wrong to say that there is a distinct absence of vitality in our poetry. All our competence with words and with craft, with images and metaphors, asks for substance; and purpose beyond mere versification is what is called for. Our poetry must be involved with us, with the many lives we live. Perhaps our prose just possesses that; it makes us participate in the myth-processes of our people—and this aspect accounts for its success in the present day." *(Journal of Indian Writing in English,* January, 2000: 5)

That is what he does in his own poetry. First, he does not lose touch with his native tradition and secondly, he is involved with the contemporary society by watching its ways from close quarters—he does not run away from reality but faces it with courage and conviction. Thus, his poetry becomes authentic of the lives and people described in it. His characters are real people in flesh and blood whom we encounter in our daily life and they speak to us in our own situation. His poetry makes us feel and see into life of things and evokes a kind of empathy between the characters and the readers. It is in this sense, Mahapatra reminds us of the great Irish Poet, W.B. Yeats. Mahapatra is deeply rooted in his soil and at the same time like a true post-colonial poet; he also writes about other people in different parts of the country and the world. If post-coloniality is another name for globalisation, Mahapatra achieves it, though in a limited scale, in his poetry.

In recent years, Mahapatra made certain pronouncements about his own poetry, which seem to me a little disturbing. 'My writing would go on to portray cultural values native to Orissa, not to other regions of India. And perhaps I have done just this in my poetry',[27] Mahapatra stated in 1994. And again he is on record to say that he is basically 'an Oriya poet who incidentally writes in English' and his poetry could be treated as 'translations'.[28] True, Mahapatra has published four volumes of poetry in Oriya since 1993. But to say that he is an Oriya poet writing in English will be a travesty of truth. In that case, Kamala Das will be a Kerali Poet, Parthasarathy, a Tamil poet, Ramanujan, a Kannada poet writing in English. Indian English is a Pan Indian language and Indian English literature, a Pan Indian Literature—perhaps the only Indian literature after Sanskrit. Jayanta Mahapatra is the first Indian English poet to win the Central Sahitya Akademi Award for his book of verse, *Relationship* in 1981. He has made a name in our country and abroad as an Indian English poet (or in recent critical terminology a post-colonial poet) but not as an Oriya poet. We may say that he is a bilingual poet and writer (for he writes Short Story in English and occasionally in Oriya) like many bilingual poets and writers in our country. Kamala Das, Manoj Das and a few others are also bilingual writers. They write in their mother tongue as well as in English. Jayanta Mahapatra like his fellow post-colonial poets A.K. Ramanujan and Shiv K. Kumar, is a translator. Nissim Ezekiel too, is a translator. We can take Jayanta Mahapatra as a bilingual poet, writer and translator. But he is first and foremost an Indian English poet (a post-colonial poet) who is read along with other post-colonial poets like Ezekiel, Kumar, Ramanujan, Daruwalla and others at home and Derek Walcott, Margaret Atwood, A.D. Hope, Judith Wright, Christopher Okigbo, Gabriel Okara and others abroad.

Speaking of the depiction of culture in his poetry, we can say that though he has largely dealt with Orissan culture in his poetry, Indian myths and topography are not missing in his poetry. For example, he writes about the 'myth of golden deer' taken from the *Ramayan,* 'the Putana myth' taken from the *Mahabharata* and Himalaya peak, which is supposed to be the abode of gods in his poetry. Indian myths, taken from the epics are employed successfully in his poetry. About contemporary society, Mahapatra writes on Bhopal gas tragedy, Punjab violence and so on. Thus, he is truly an Indian poet writing in English language that at once qualifies him to be an Indian English poet and according to the recent critical parlance, he is a post-colonial poet, 'who himself is the unity of his work'.

## NOTES

1. Bruce King, *Modern Indian Poetry in English,* Delhi: Oxford University Press, 1987, pp. 194-95.
2. John Oliver Perry, "Neither Alien nor Post-Modern: Jayanta Mahapatra's Poetry from India", *The Kenyon Review*, VoI. VIII, No. 4, Fall, 1986, p. 56.
3. Jayanta Mahapatra, *Contemporary Author Autobiography Series,* Michigan, Vol. 9, p. 148.
4. John Oliver Perry, "Neither Alien nor Post-modern: Jayanta Mahapatra's Poetry from India", *The Kenyon Review,* Vol. VIII, No. 4, Fall, 1986, 61.
5. Jayanta Mahapatra, *Contemporary Author Autobiography Series,* Michigan, Vol. 9, p. 149.
6. Jayanta Mahapatra, *The Illustrated Weekly of India,* April 1, 1990, p. 30.
7. *Ibid.*, 7.
8. Jayanta Mahapatra, *A Whiteness of Bone,* New Delhi: Penguin Books India, 1992, 35.
9. Quoted by Bruce King, "The Shaper of Solitude", *The Poetry of Jayanta Mahapatra: A Critical Study,* (ed.) Madhusudan Prasad (New Delhi: Sterling Publishers Pvt. Ltd., 1986), p. 18.

10. *Ibid.*, pp. 18-19.
11. Jayanta Mahapatra, "The Measure of Mystery in Poetry", *Journal of Literary Studies,* Vol. 10, No. 1, 1987, p. 44.
12. *Ibid.*, p. 46.
13. S.K. Desai, "The Poetic Craft", *The Poetry of Jayanta Mahapatra: A Critical Study,* p. 127.
14. Alan Kennedy, "Written Rites", *The Poetry of Jayanta Mahapatra: A Critical Study,* p. 82.
15. Quoted by Norman Simms, "A Poet of Many Worlds", *The Poetry of Jayanta Mahapatra: A Critical Study,* pp. 33-34.
16. *Ibid.*, p. 35.
17. *Ibid.*, p. 31.
18. Jayanta Mahapatra, *The Illustrated Weekly of India,* April 1, 1990, p. 30.
19. G.S. Fraser, *The Modern Writer and His World* (Baltimore: Penguin Books, 1970), p. 11.
20. R.J. Quinones, *Mapping Literary Modernism: Time and Development* (Princeton: Princeton University Press, 1985), p. 3.
21. *Ibid.*, pp. 255-56.
22. Quoted by Syed Amanuddin, *World Poetry in English* (New Delhi: Sterling Publishers, 1981), p. 52.
23. R.J. Quinones, *Mapping Literary Modernism: Time and Development,* p. 193.
24. Notes to the Poem, *The Temple,* p. 57.
25. R.J. Quinones, *Mapping Literary Modernism,* p. 4.
26. John Oliver Perry, "Working Conditions of Indian English Poets as compared with their American Counterparts", *Kavyabharati*, No.2, 1989, p. 60.
27. Jayanta Mahapatra, "Mystery as Mantra: Letter from Orissa", *World Literature Today* (Spring, 1994): 288.
28. Vilas Sarang, Quoted, ed. 'Introduction', *Indian English Poetry Since 1950 : An Anthology,* (Bombay: Disha, 1990) : 32.

# Jayanta Mahapatra in Conversation with Bijay Kumar Das*

9

(Recipient of the first ever Sahitya Akademi Award for Indian English Poetry for his book of verse, *Relationship* for 1981, Jayanta Mahapatra is India's best known poet abroad. He has sixteen books of poetry in English (the last being *Random Descent* 2005), eight books of Poetry Translation, a collection of short stories, a book of prose titled, *Door of Paper* (2007) to his credit. He won several awards at home and abroad. Utkal University, Bhubaneswar conferred on him D. Litt (Honoris Causa) in recognition of his contribution to Indian Literature in 2006)

***BKD*:** I would like to begin by quoting the opening sentence of your latest book, *Door of Paper,* "There is a door in the heart of man which never opens" and asking you to open it for a while. Could you please tell me about the atmosphere in which you grew up during your childhood days?

***JM*:** In the brief autobiographical piece I wrote for the Gale *Contemporary Authors Autobiography Series* (1989) I did mention about the pain that goes with childhood. At least there was some pain in mine. But I have talked about this a number of times and it is turning into a cliche. The point is, beginning with childhood, as one grows up, the outer world affects him much. It is hard to come to terms with the indignities, the cruelties he faces for no fault of his. And if you are somewhat shy, this takes on huge proportions. I suppose one has to find solace in some corner of his own. And then, perhaps both outside and inside yourself, the "door" never opens. This much I can say now: I was never comfortable at home. My father was away most of the time, and

---

* This interview was first published in *The Indian Journal of English Studies* Vol.45, Jan. 2008.

there was my mother and younger brother. The unhappiness at home smothered me. To confess, I ran away from home twice, but eventually came back. I don't wish to speak about this past now.

***BKD*:** You had your education in English Medium School and were fond of fiction in your school days. How did you start writing poetry?

***JM*:** Well, perhaps I would never have gone into poetry. I don't know. Fiction has always interested me, and all my spare hours went into the reading of novels. This became a strong habit. I haven't been able to give up. Reading is fascinating, besides the good it is supposed to do. Maybe I thought I would write novels when I grew up. But that did not happen. When I began to write at first, and I was twenty one, I started with fiction. But the stories I sent out came back with rejection slips. I realized painfully I was destined not to be a writer. It hurt. But there are many things in the world one can do. I could savour life at its fullest. I had never ever imagined I would be able to write poetry one day. I was aging fast.

And poetry. This came to me much later, when I was approaching forty—an age when poets have finished their strongest work. But some things happen in life and reasons are not always easy to find. Something could have triggered my emotions, and I was swept along this new, strange path. When I sent my new, fumbling creations to different periodicals, I found some were accepted. It gave me a direction for living.

***BKD*:** You began publishing your book of poems in the nineteen seventies. How did you feel when your poems were published abroad in literary magazines like *Chicago Review, New York Quarterly, Poetry* and *Sewanee Review* in U.S.A., and *Critical Quarterly* and the *Times Literary Supplement* in England?

***JM*:** It was like treading on unchartered territory. These were significant periodicals in which the best in England and USA published, so the satisfaction was immense. Here I was a physics man, and then I lived in a remote place in India, away from the standard centres of English poetry. The publications brought me a sense of confidence I had sorely missed in life. I knew I could write poetry.

***BKD*:** I think your fourth volume of poems, *A Rain of Rites* is a turning point in your career as a poet. Your reactions, please.

***JM*:** Yes, it was a turning point in my poetic career; I'm sorry I missed that until you pointed it out to me. *A Rain of Rites* was published by the University of Georgia Press, USA, in 1976, and was my first volume of poetry to be published by an American University Press. The manuscript was selected from a large number of manuscripts submitted to the Press, and both readers' and the editor's comments were really good. It was on a hunch that I had submitted the manuscript to The University of Georgia Press, and to have your book win this poetry contest was something unforgettable—more so because I lived here in Cuttack and had no contacts with the centres of poetry. And this too, after reviews of my first two books in India were damning. I had no encouragement at all from my peers in India. It was just my will to write well that led me on. It was a good feeling. Later on, some excellent reviews of this book appeared in places like *The Hudson Review*. It gave a boost to my career.
*BKD*: How did you feel when you were given the prestigious Jacob Glatstein Memorial Prize in 1975?

***JM*:** Living alone, here in Cuttack, with nobody to help me with my craft, the news of the Award reassured me as nothing else could. I knew that I could write, and write well. The Award was given for eleven poems of mine that had appeared in *POETRY Magazine* in the year—in two instalments, there were 4 poems in one issue and 7 poems in another. It was something for me to be happy about. It made me really happy.

***BKD*:** Mid-nineteen seventies seem to be the blossoming of your talent as a poet. You were chosen by Paul Engle, the Director of the International Writing Program at Iowa for the year 1976-77. What was your reaction then?

***JM*:** Yes, the mid-seventies were good for me. To publish seven poems in one group in *POETRY* was something that never happens every day. *The Sewanee Review* published 4 poems that very year, I think, and I could feel the momentum of these publications. And when the Director of the International Writing Program at Iowa, Paul Engle, sent me an invitation to attend the Program for 1976-77, I was thrilled. More so because I had not applied, nor did I know anything about this Program. Paul had invited me to Iowa on the basis of the Jacob Glatstein Award and because of the poems that had appeared in significant Journals in the United States. I was truly happy.

***BKD***: Do you believe that writing poetry can be taught in the true sense of the term?

***JM***: The answer to your question would be "No." None of the great poets had ever attended a creative writing class. Poetry is a subjective response. Certainly there are bound to be influences in one's poetry, but eventually one gets over them and develops one's own. When I was in the Program at Iowa, I had the opportunity to attend a couple of creative writing classes, but I didn't find anything to excite me. The results of these classes were monochromatically uniform. I remember the American poet, Rita Dove was there, and she went on to win the Pulitzer Prize for poetry after some years.

***BKD***: It is true that your poetry was accepted and appreciated in the West much before it was recognised in India. Did anyone in India encourage you to write and publish poems?

***JM***: Perhaps I wasn't writing that kind of poetry which academics and editors would encourage. My poems were complex, and their abstract quality deterred them. I think I can't say. But I didn't get any encouragement here in my country. On the other hand, editors like Professor C.B. Cox of the *Critical Quarterly* wrote to me that it was the first time he had published anyone from India. Again, it was the Winter 1974 issue of the CQ where he published 7 of my poems.

***BKD:*** Let me turn to your poetry. In India, Indian English poets are broadly divided into two categories: One, those who identify themselves with the landscape of the place and contemporary India, and two, those who acclimatize the indigenous tradition to English language. I think you belong to both the categories. What do you say?

***JM***: Look, I live in Orissa. So it is but natural that I write about what I see and what I hear and feel. There is nothing else to my poetry. I haven't studied any poetry so I would know what I am doing. It is the place which chooses me to write, because I live here, and the air of the place is under my skin. That's all. I'm sorry I cannot talk about categories. As a critic you have to decide which of these two categories suits my poetry. Or whether I belong to both categories.

***BKD***: Tradition, history, myth—all these form the thematic content of your poetry. *Relationship* is a milestone in Indian English Poetry. No wonder that it earned you the first ever Sahitya Akademi Award (National Academy) in 1981. On receiving the Award you said: "To Orissa, to this land in which my roots lie and lies my past, and in which lies my beginning and my end, where the wind keens over the great grief of the River Daya and where the waves of the Bay of Bengal fail to reach out today to the twilight soul of Konarka, I acknowledge my debt and relationship". My question is, like T.S. Eliot, do you emphasize 'time' and 'history' in your poetry?

***JM***: I should like to answer your question by stressing what poetry does, and not by *my* pursuits in my poetry. Great poetry has always chosen and preserved experience, and this is not something easy to achieve. As a poet one tries to do this, to give life to what has touched him most in myth or legend or even, fact, and bringing these into timeless proportions. But as I said, this is difficult. Perhaps in this way poetry helps to protect our civilization; this urge to preserve the past and also to look into the future becomes a true requisite for good poetry everywhere. Poetry's concern is with the art of life, to provide us with the means to live fully and truthfully. So, as a poet, how could I not be conscious of my past and of the history which has shaped me, both personal and racial? I suppose any feeling Oriya would be moved by the massacre of a hundred thousand Oriyas in the war which Asoka waged against our fore-fathers in 261 BC? Therefore, isn't it but natural that I should make poetry out of these historic happenings? So also about society which has influenced my consciousness and my life?

Emphasizing history is but natural; it shows how the bones of history are made up of time.

*BKD*: There are a number of ways in which a poet can give a distinct touch and an identity to his poetry. He can do it by acclimatizing an indigenous tradition to a language other than one's first language (in your case, English) and by way of evocating the place to which he belongs. This commitment to locale is seen in the poetry of Robert Frost (New England), W.B. Yeats (Sligo), Nissim Ezekiel (Bombay, Now 'Mumbai'). Can we take the golden triangle—Cuttack, Bhubaneswar and Puri—as the locale of your poetry?

*JM*: This place, Orissa, its earth, its air—all of these have shaped my growing up. So I would write about it, which I do. Orissa is for me an exciting and attractive field of a sensibility. Instinctively I write about the traditions, the myths and the history of Orissa. And this local colour is very important for me; it is the local which powers me into new outlooks and ideas.

Of course, Cuttack, Bhubaneswar and Puri are near to me; but probably nearer emotionally than their geographical distances. My personal history has something to do with this. And my own makeup, my growing up in the rural Cuttack of my childhood which was just a weedy, malarial, overgrown village. But I would say the whole land of Orissa sustains me and my poetry. Take this land away, and I'd be lost somewhere!

*BKD*: You have written sixteen books of poems and never looked back since you received the Sahitya Akademi Award in 1981. You have a great sense of movement in your poetry. You write poems about the past and present (i.e, the contemporary scene). Do you look at the world as a flux that undergoes changes from moment to moment?

*JM*: Of course. This movement, seen or unseen, hangs there, in front of you, behind you, breaking and building your dreams. Eventually your life and your poetry. The movement is hard to see: at times it breathes blood, it does not allow us to distinguish human beings from animals. I suppose this chaos seeps into one's poems.

*BKD*: In your essay, "Face to Face with the Contemporary poem", you have written that, "the relation between a poem and reader is a reversible process, a two-way affair". Would you kindly elaborate it?

***JM*:** I'd like to think that a poem hasn't done what it is supposed to do unless it touches a reader. If the poem is left to itself unattended on a page, unread, then the poem is almost meaningless. But if its reading touches a reader, and he is moved by the feeling (and language) in the poem, it has done its work. I didn't have any high and mighty ideas in mind when I said that the relation is "a reversible process." I simply wanted to stress that a poem should be able to *move* the reader, similar to the charge accumulating in a condenser—which only if it is enough, can pass over to the other plate of the condenser as an electric spark, enabling the process between reader and poet to be complete. Therefore, the strength of the poem supports the reverse process.

***BKD*:** Poetry is broadly divided into two types: "Direct poetry" and "Oblique poetry". 'Direct Poetry' is that kind of poetry in which the surface meaning is the meaning of it, while in 'Oblique poetry' one thing is stated in terms of another (ie, through images, metaphor and symbols). Which kind of poetry do you write?

***JM*:** My preference is for poetry which uses symbols, metaphors and images to state the poem's concerns. Not that I have anything against direct statement in poetry, but I like to use or write "oblique poetry" (your words). It's my choice. But if I could, I'd write both types of poetry.

***BKD*:** In your essay, "Freedom as Poetry: The Door", you have stated that; "one tends to feel that there are two kinds of poetry being written today, in almost all countries of the world—the one which caters more or less to the establishment, and which is relatively safe poetry because it carries no sort of risk or danger to the poet. The other, and this type of verse has been written in other times as well and in many places including our own, becomes a dangerous occupation—because generally such poetry is critical of the establishment and therefore is against the well being of the poet". The statement seems to be true. Which kind of poetry do you prefer?

*JM*: Look, it's not a question of writing safe poetry or anti-establishment poetry. One doesn't deliberately do such things. If one comes across injustice or unnecessary violence in the society in which the poet lives, then one is forced to write about this. I write about whatever hurts me, social or political.

*BKD*: In *Silence: Poetry's Last Word*, you have stated that "a poet, is first of all responsible to his or her own conscience, otherwise he or she cannot be called a poet". Do you mean to say that the poet has to be honest to himself or herself?

*JM*: This is what I believe in: That a poet, first of all, should be responsible to his or her own conscience. In other words, the poet should be basically honest. At times, one feels, romanticism could lead the poet toward a kind of insincerity, which does not seem proper for poetry. Let the poet not succumb to the superficiality of poetry, abandoning himself to a false sincerity where the poetry loses its value. It is but proper that the poet should look at the world with his inner conscience and talk about those things which he feels mar it. I feel that way. I would like to make myself worthy of poetry. I try, but I can't say what I have been.

*BKD*: You have written a few poems on Gandhi. Do you intend to create a living myth out of Gandhi, as R.K. Narayan, Mulk Raj Anand and Raja Rao have done in fiction?

*JM*: No, there's no question of making a myth of Gandhi. I have immense regard for him, having grown up with his thoughts, and his courage has been exemplary. One usually does not come across that sort of courage today. To go to a Round Table Conference in Britain, clad in a thin dhoti, takes on high and noble proportions. I could never do that, but wear my best suit to sit with all those people. And then, I was fortunate to attend his prayer meetings at the Bankipur Maidan in Patna, where I was studying for my M.Sc. There is so much to be learnt from his life. Regard for him has come about naturally. My writing is not deliberate.

*BKD*: You have written a poem, "Madhuri Dixit" in *Random Descent* (2005). Do you want to emphasize the dance tradition of our country through her character?

***JM*:** Look, 1 am a simple man. Madhuri Dixit held audiences in sway with her looks and her acting. It was but natural that I admire her. And it is a consequence of this admiration that I wrote this poem to her. She was all woman. The dance tradition of which you speak did not enter my mind.

***BKD*:** Some lines of your poetry seem to be prophetic. Take for instance, the line "But life is always something else" ("Re - enacting an Old Play"). Would you please explain that line?

***JM*:** Prophetic? Well, I can't answer that. Take the human mind, for example. It is packed with feelings we know nothing about, besides other unknowns: like images of people we have never seen, sounds of voices we've never heard, and places we have never ever visited. So it is extremely difficult to give a precise or absolute meaning to any of our thoughts or actions. Can I say that poetry is the end all in my life? It is not mathematics that I would insist: This only is what matters to me in life. I would like to believe life is something else besides the statements I make at times in my poems. And this is true. The workings of the brain are so complex that it is hard to make generalisations, and order is not easy to achieve.

***BKD*:** Having asked you a few questions on your poetry, let me turn to other aspects. That is, who are the writers and poets you admire?

***JM*:** I can single out poets who are writing in different languages, writers from various countries—whose poems have come to me in English translation. Among novelists I would mention Jose Saramago, Garcia Marquez, Haruki Murakami, Elias Canetti; there are many others. Among poets, there are Salvatore Quasimodo, Cesar Vallejo, Pablo Neruda, to name a few. Well, there are so many who I look up to; it's difficult to give names.

***BKD*:** What do you think about the reviewing of your books in India and abroad?

***JM*:** I'd say this much: I have had more problems getting my books reviewed in India than in other foreign countries. But some of the fine reviews have been in the United States. I don't know if you remember the review that appeared in 1978 (I think)—of *A Rain of Rites* in *The Hudson Review,* and it was done by the critic Vernon Young. It really gave me new life!

But I got scathing reviews of my first two volumes of poetry. Even *Relationship* got a damaging review in the Sahitya Akademi Journal, *Indian Literature.* Well, my luck! On the other hand, I've been fortunate in getting letters from some editors in the US. I'd like to mention Goorge Core, Editor of *The Sewanee Review,* Brian Cox, Poetry Editor of *Critical Quarterly,* and from the Poetry Editor, *The New Yorker*—who have been publishing me regularly through the years; their letters have always inspired me.

***BKD*:** Now there are quite a few books on your poetry (both written and edited). Do you think these books really help the readers in understanding your poetry?

***JM*:** The books should be of help. My poems are generally thought of to be abstruse, and not many students or readers would have the patience to read them. Certainly, yes. These books should help readers.

***BKD*:** After having achieved success as an Indian English poet, you have started writing poetry in your first language (i.e, Oriya). Why did you turn to writing poetry in Oriya?

***JM*:** I had been writing poetry for about twenty five years or more in English before I thought of starting out in my mother tongue, Oriya. Frankly, my experience with English poems had revealed that local colors hadn't got into the poems. I felt I could speak in a more colloquial manner if I wrote poetry in Oriya. And then, I thought the common man would read my work; the fast-food vendor for instance, or the boiled-egg seller. It was a sort of challenge, and I am happy I took it up. I discovered too that the English and Oriya poems complemented each other; there were certain poems I could have written in Oriya alone. The fact remains; I am an Oriya poet, whichever language I might use.

***BKD*:** You have achieved numerous awards both at home and abroad. Are you really affected by them?

***JM*:** A few awards, yes. The answer is NO.

***BKD*:** The last question. Apart from poetry, you also write short story and essays. Your latest book, *Door of Paper*: *Essays and Memoirs* came out in 2007. How would you like to be described: an Indian English poet and writer, a bilingual poet and writer or an Indian poet and writer?

***JM*:** I suppose the label of an Indian poet would suit me. That's all.

# Bibliography


***Primary Sources***

Mahapatra, Jayanta. *Close the Sky, Ten by Ten.* Calcutta: Dialogue Publications, 1971.

——, *Svayamvara and Other Poems.* Calcutta: Writers Workshop, 1971.

——, *A Father's Hours,* Calcutta: United Writers, 1976.

——, *A Rain of Rites,* Athens: University of Georgia Press, 1976.

——, *Waiting,* New Delhi: Samakaleen Prakashan, 1975.

——, *The False Start,* Bombay: Clearing House, 1980.

——, *Relationship,* Greenfield, New York: Greenfield Review Press, 1980.

——, *Life Signs,* New Delhi: Oxford University Press, 1983.

——, *Dispossessed Nests,* Jaipur: Nirala Publications, 1986.

——, *Selected Poems,* New Delhi: Oxford University Press, 1987.

——, *Burden of Waves and Fruit.* Washington, D.C.: Three Continents Press, 1988.

——, *Temple,* Sydney: Dangaroo Press, 1989.

——, *A Whiteness of Bone,* New Delhi: Penguin Books, 1992.

——, *The Best of Jayanta Mahapatra,* Calicut. Bodhi Books, 1995.

——, *Shadow Space*, Kottayam: D.C. Books, 1997.

——, *Bare Face*, Kottayam: D.C. Books, 2000.

*Secondary Sources*

——, *Random Descent*. Bhubaneswar: Third Eye Communications, 2005.

**Articles**

Allen, Frank, "Crisis of Belief', Parnassus (Spring/Summer 1981) : 333-42.

Chari, Jaganmohan A., 'The Logic' As Jayanta Mahapatra's Poetic", *Kakatiya Journal of English Studies:* 5, 1983.

Das, Bijay Kumar, "Journey into the Unknown: Jayanta Mahapatra's 'Relationship'." *The Humanities Review*: 5, 1983, pp. 5-7.

——, "Post-1960 Indian English Poetry and the Making of Indian English Idiom." *Indian English Literature Since Independence,* (ed.) K. Ayyappapaniker (New Delhi: Indian Association for English Studies, 1990) : 115-23.

——, "The Image of the Native Land in the Award Winning Poets", Chairoscuro, (ed.), A.S. Ratnam (Parbhani: Dnyanopasak Prakashan), 1991 : 25-37.

——, "Indian English Poetry: Retrospect and Prospect", *The Commonwealth Review,* 5 : 1, 1994.

——, "Akademi Award Winning Indian English Poetry as Post-colonial Text", *Critical Practice* 6 : 2, 1999.

——, "Orissan Contribution to Indian English Literature", *The Continuity in the Flux,* (eds.) Dinanath Pathy and Ramesh P. Panigrahi. New Delhi: Harman Publishing House, 1999.

Mahapatra, Jayanta, "The Decline of Indian English Poetry", *The Journal of Indian Writing in English,* 28 : 1, 2000.

Mishra, Soubhagya, K., "The Largest Circle: A Reading of Jayanta Mahapatra's 'Relationship'," *The Literary Endeavour*: 9 (1-4); 1987-88 : 30-48.

Mohanty, Niranjan, "Recollection as Redemption: Poetry of Jayanta Mahapatra", *Poetry*: 10; 1985.

Naik, M.K., 'Only Connect', Indian Book Chronicle, January 1982.

Nayar, Pramod K., "Poetry of the Nineties", *Chandrabhaga,* 1/ 2000 : 95-119.

Paniker, Ayyappa K., "The Poetry of Jayanta Mahapatra", *Osmania Journal of English Studies*: 13 : 1; 1977 : 117-38.

Perry, John Oliver, "Neither Alien nor Post-modern Jayanta Mahapatra's Poetry from India," *The Kenyon Review,* 8 : 4, Fall, 1986.

Prasad, Madhusudan, "Caught in the Currents of Time: A Study of the Poetry of Jayanta Mahapatra", *Journal of South-Asian Literature*: 19 : 2 : 1984.

Ramanan, Mohan, "The Script and the Body: Contemporary Indian Poetry in English and the Colonial Context", *Journal of Indian Writing in English* 25 : 1-2, 1997.

Rath, Harihar, "Life Against Ruins: A Study of Jayanta Mahapatra's 'The False Start'", *Indian Scholar*: 3 : 1 : January, 1981.

Raveendran, P.P., "Decolonising Indian English Poetry", Introduction, ed. *The Best of Jayanta Mahapatra,* Calicut: Bodhi Books, 1955.

Rayan, Krishna, "Contemporary Indian English Poetry and the Gods", *Chandrabhaga,* 1/2000 : 43-52.

Shahane, V.A., '"The Naked Earth and Beyond: The Poetry of Jayanta Mahapatra", *Perspectives on Indian Poetry in English* (ed.) M.K. Naik, New Delhi: Abhinav Publications, 1984.

Swain, Rabindra K., "A Voice of Humility: The Poetry of Jayanta Mahapatra". *Indian Literature*: 26 : 1, 1983.

Tarinayya, M., "Jayanta Mahapatra's Letter to Shiraishi in Tokyo: An Analysis", *The Literary Criterion* 20 : 3, 1985.

### Books

Abidi, S.Z.H., *Studies in Indo-Anglian Poetry*, Bareilly: Prakash Book Depot, 1978.

Daruwalla, Keki N., ed., *Two Decades of Indian Poetry,* 1960-80. New Delhi: Vikas Publishing House, 1980.

Das, Bijay Kumar, *Modern Indo-English Poetry,* Bareilly: Prakash Book Depot, 1982.

——, (ed.), *Contemporary Indo-English Poetry,* Bareilly: Prakash Book Depot, 1986.

——, *Critical Perspective on 'Relationship' and Latter-Day Psalms,* Bareilly: Prakash Book Depot, 1986.

——, *Modern Indian English Poetry,* Bareilly: PBD, 1992.

——, *A Reader's Guide to 'Ten Twentieth Century Indian Poets',* Bareilly: PBD, 1993.

——, *Perspectives on Indian English Poetry Criticism,* Bareilly: PBD, 1993.

——, *Critical Essays on Poetry,* New Delhi: Kalyani Publishers, 1993, 2003.

——, *Aspects of Commonwealth Literature,* New Delhi: Creative Books, 1995.

——, *Critical Essays on Post-colonial Literature,* New Delhi: Atlantic Publishers, 1999, 2nd edition. 2007.

——, *Post-modern Indian English Literature*, New Delhi: Atlantic, 2006

King, Bruce, *Modern Indian Poetry in English,* New Delhi: Oxford University Press, 1987.

Kulshrestha, Chirantan, ed. *Contemporary Indian English Verse: An Evaluation,* New Delhi: Arnold Heinemann, 1980.

Naik, M.K., *Dimensions of Indian English Literature,* New Delhi: Sterling Publishers, 1984.

——, *A History of Indian English Literature,* New Delhi: Sahitya Akademi, 1982.

——, *Studies in Indian English Literature,* New Delhi: Sterling Publishers, 1987.

——, (ed.) *Perspectives of Indian Poetry in English,* New Delhi: Abhinav Publications, 1984.

——, *et al,* (ed.), *Critical Essays on Indian Writing in English,* Dharwar: Karnatak University, 1968.

Paranjape, Makarand P., *Mysticism in Indian English Poetry,* Delhi: B.R. Publication, 1988.

Paniker, K. Ayyappa ed., *Modern Indian Poetry in English,* New Delhi: Sahitya Akademi, 1991.

——, ed. *Indian English Literature Since Independence,* New Delhi: Indian Association for English Studies, 1990.

Parthasarathy, R., ed., *The Twentieth Century Indian Poets,* New Delhi: Oxford University Press, 1977.

Pathak, R.S. ed., *Quest for Identity,* New Delhi: Bahri Publications, 1992.

Patke, Rajeev S. *Postcolonial Poetry in English*, New Delhi: Oxford University Press, 2007.

Prasad, Madhusudan, ed., *The Poetry of Jayanta Mahapatra: A Critical Study.* New Delhi: Sterling Publishers Pvt. Ltd., 1986.

Sarang, Vilas, ed., *Indian English Poetry Since 1950: An Anthology,* Bombay: Disha Books, 1995.

Shahane, Vasant A. and Sivaram Krishana, M. (eds.), *Indian Poetry in English: A Critical Assessment,* Madras: MacMillan, 1982.

Walsh, William, *Indian Literature in English,* London: Longman, 1990.

# Index